GOLF'S
GOLDEN RULE

GOLF'S GOLDEN RULE

WHAT EVERY PRO DOES INSTINCTIVELY... AND YOU DON'T

STEVE GOULD & D.J. WILKINSON

First published 2012 by Elliott and Thompson Ltd

27 John Street, London WC1N 2BX

www.eandtbooks.com

ISBN 978-1-907642-54-8

Text copyright © Steve Gould and D.J. Wilkinson

Studio and school photographs by Mark Barton

Competition and course photographs © Charles Briscoe-Knight

9 8 7 6 5 4 3 2 1

A CIP catalogue record for this book is available from the British Library

Designed by Jon Wainwright

Printed in Italy by Printer Trento on sustainable paper.

FSC
www.fsc.org
MIX
Paper from
responsible sources
FSC® C015829

CONTENTS

We would like to thank:

Tony Lawrence, Phil Talbot, David Lamplough, Mark Barton,

Charles Briscoe-Knight, Peter Kershaw, Barry O'Brian,

Darrell Bennett, Vic Parnis, Ian Bloom, SilverCut Productions,

John Lord, Bronagh Woods, Jon Wainwright, Lorne Forsyth,

Olivia Bays, Nick Sidwell and Alison Menzies.

USEFUL EQUIPMENT FOR THIS BOOK

There are Best Practice sections throughout this book containing exercises that you can do to improve and maintain your swing. You may also wish to follow some or all of the other routines we describe. In order to be best prepared, you will find the following household items and pieces of standard golfing equipment helpful:

- A golf club, preferably an iron as they are easier to swing in an average home.

- An impact bag, available from all good golf stores and pro shops. You can also improvise with an old holdall.

- An empty grip, available from all golf stores and pro shops. Alternatively, your local pro shop may cut down an old club for you. If they do so, ask for a couple of inches of shaft to be left below the grip. In place of either of these, a small-scale children's club would work.

- A frying pan or a tennis racquet!

- A full-length mirror.

INTRODUCTION

WHAT EVERY PRO
DOES INSTINCTIVELY...
AND YOU DON'T

WHAT EVERY PRO DOES INSTINCTIVELY... AND YOU DON'T

Next time you go to a professional golf tournament, arrive early and head for the practice range. Watch closely. You'll see something fascinating.

Most of the top players open their warm-up sessions with a ritual so innocuous that it fails to register with onlookers. Selecting a short iron, they peer down the range while making a series of miniature swings. The club is swung back and through, brushing the grass on the way. It's almost as if they're searching for something.

Go to your local range and you'll see something quite different. There, players begin with full swings – often with the driver – while checking their alignment or looking over their shoulder to admire the top of their backswing. There's nothing wrong, of course, with big practice swings or with checking your alignment and backswing. There's logic to it. But it's not what the pros do.

"Impact should not be left as a blur. Impact is the moment that decides where the ball will go, at what trajectory and at what speed. It is the one moment during your swing when club makes contact with ball."

So what are they up to?

Simply put, they're reacquainting themselves with impact and the impact zone.

It's obvious, once you give it some thought. The impact zone – an area measuring a couple of feet before the ball and a couple after it – is what good golf is all about. It's sometimes referred to as the 'business end' of the golf swing. As such, it should be analysed, understood and practised more than anything else.

But it isn't.

Work your way through most golf instruction and you'll find that impact barely warrants a mention – not in any detailed sense, anyway. You're told to get your hands ahead of the ball and hit down. You're told divots are good. And that's about it.

Millions of words have been written on grip, alignment, posture and set-up, on shoulder turn and weight shift. Entire books have been devoted to the power of positive thinking. Clearly, these are important factors. Many, indeed, are fundamental. As golf teachers, we spend a great deal of time building or reshaping our students' backswings. That will never change. A structured backswing, downswing and throughswing are all close relations of the impact zone.

But the importance of impact seems to have got lost in golf's ever-increasing mountains of detail. As everyone stampedes in search of the sport's next 'Big Idea', impact has been passed by. It has become just another fleeting moment, a millisecond, a blink of an eye, to be squeezed in somewhere between perfect backswings and picture-postcard finishes.

Ask most players at your club what they're working on and you can guarantee that no one will mention impact.

Impact just happens, doesn't it?

It's an understandable reaction. Impact is a mystery to the majority of golfers, even very good players. Good players rely on instinct. Few of them are able to explain exactly what their hands and arms do as the club travels at 100 mph through the impact zone. 'I just hit it,' they'll tell you. And that is exactly what they do. They are the lucky, naturally talented few.

For lesser golfers, though, impact gets lost in a red mist of frustration and misplaced optimism.

Until recently, video had not been sophisticated enough to isolate the key moments of impact in single frames, offering instead a blur of hands and club. That made it very hard to dissect what is happening. Many teachers, pressurised by their pupils' impatience to get out and play, choose to brush the impact zone under the carpet.

After all, impact just happens, doesn't it?

No.

Impact should not be left as a blur. It is not a moment. It is The Moment. Impact is the moment that decides where the ball will go, at what trajectory and at what speed. It is the one moment during your swing when club makes contact with ball.

Which is why the impact zone represents the heart of this book.

We will, of course, continue into the backswing on the one side, and the finish on the other. For 99 out of 100 golfers, these must be mastered as well. Take the backswing. Only the most mercurial of players can merge an eccentric backswing with a great impact. For the rest of us, a good, solid backswing is a prerequisite for success.

But remember. A pure ball strike is everything. That is what makes impact the moment of truth.

Technically, the golf swing may start with the set-up and end with the finish. For us, though, golf starts and ends with impact.

Impact is everything.

CHAPTER 1

THE IMPACT ZONE… AND GOLF'S GOLDEN RULE

Not all good golf swings look the same… not until, that is, they reach the impact zone. Then they are virtually identical. This is golf's 'Golden Rule'. To play great golf, you must master what happens through the hitting area.

GOLF'S GOLDEN RULE

IN THE ZONE

If a textbook impact zone forms an integral part of your swing, then you're a good golfer. And if it does not, you probably aren't.

It's that simple.

A golf swing without a textbook impact zone is, in 99 out of 100 cases, a golf swing going nowhere – or, more accurately, one heading for the long grass.

Some good players, it's true, consistently salvage their swings at the last moment and hit straight shots despite not entering the impact zone correctly. They tend to have very fine hand control, with which they subsidise the rest of their swing. And they tend to play and practise a great deal. A very great deal.

"A pure ball strike is everything.

That is what makes impact the

moment of truth."

The vast majority of golfers, though, will pull off such salvage operations only occasionally. Very occasionally. And don't be fooled when, one time out of 20, you succeed in hitting a 250-yard drive straight down the fairway or strike a 7-iron approach to 5 feet. We're sorry, but that shot does not prove that you can do it. It merely proves that you can do it ONE TIME OUT OF 20. The statistics do not lie. Your bad shots will continue to far outnumber your good.

Get into the correct position coming into impact, however, and the opposite is true. You will be perfectly placed to deliver the club face squarely into the back of the ball.

There's no way round golf's Golden Rule. A correct impact zone must form part of a good, reliable and repeatable swing.

But here's the good news. Be methodical, take one small step at a time, and it's easier to achieve than you may think.

(right)
If you've got this, you've got golf: The composite image on the right shows the full impact zone. This is what this book is about – this is Golf's Golden Rule. You can see each stage of the impact zone in greater detail in the pictures on pages 202-205.

IMPACT ZONE

THE IMPACT ZONE – STEP 1

Hit this position consistently and you'll find it hard to go wrong.

The club head and shaft are exactly where they should be. Seen sideways on, the club shaft seems to be aligned with right forearm.

THE PERFECT APPROACH TO IMPACT

Step 1 is all about learning where you must be to enter the impact zone correctly. Examine the position in the pictures to the left as the player approaches the impact zone, then try to copy it while standing in front of a full-length mirror. In fact, a full-length mirror is a prerequisite to reading and getting the most out of this book. Seeing exactly what you are doing right – and what you are doing wrong – is vital to your progress.

Here are some key checkpoints, looking at the golfer from face on. Note that, at this early stage, we are dealing with a set or 'frozen' position rather than a movement.

Your chest and shoulders are facing slightly behind the ball, while your core and hips are square, or even just beyond square, to the ball-to-target line.

Your body is balanced and centred, not sliding laterally across towards the target. Your arms are alive and active, rather than taut and tense, with plenty of space in which to swing. They form an inverted triangle with the top of the shoulders.

Your hands are just below hip height – say 8 o'clock on an imaginary clock face, as seen from face on – with your right palm facing directly away from your body. Check this crucial hand position closely with the pictures. The palm is not facing the ball.

It's almost as if you are shaking the hand of somebody standing directly to your right. This palm position will be mirrored by the club face – it too is not yet facing the ball. Your wrists are hinged upwards, forming a 90-degree angle between your forearms and club shaft. The club head is above your wrists.

Your upper arms are touching the sides of your chest. Note that your right elbow is pointing towards your right hip, while the inside of your right elbow joint, like the palm of the right hand, is facing directly in front of you, away from your body.

Now let us view things along the ball-to-target line, as shown in the righthand picture on the opposite page.

Your left bicep is touching the left side of your chest. The club head, as already noted, is above your wrists. Seen from this angle, the club shaft forms a 45-degree angle between the horizontal and vertical – or, put another way, the shaft seems to run down the right forearm.

You are now perfectly positioned – you are in 'the slot' – as you enter the impact zone. You cannot practise this position too much.

THE IMPACT ZONE – STEP 2

THE MAGIC OF RELEASE

Master step 1 of the impact zone and you will be ready for step 2 – an action which 9 out of 10 golfers never understand, let alone achieve.

The 'release' has earned an almost mythical status among high-handicappers. They regard it as a mysterious, magical move that good players have harnessed to produce extra power and precision.

Release, however, does not need to be mysterious – even though it will indeed have a magical effect on your ball striking.

When most people refer to it, they mean 'hand release' (there is also a 'body release', which we will explain later).

Hand release is an action which allows the shaft, and thus the club head, to accelerate dramatically through the impact zone. It also makes it possible to square the club, in the simplest way possible.

So you are swinging down into the impact zone. It is now time to fit in your new hand action.

THE KEY CHECKPOINTS

It's easier to identify hand release viewed from along the ball-to-target line. First let us repeat and re-emphasise the key checkpoints as you enter the impact zone. Don't rush. These checkpoints are your route to success.

Your arms are swinging down, with the hands reaching hip level. Seen from face on, there is a 90-degree angle between your forearms and club shaft.

Seen from along the ball-to-target line, the shaft seems to run down the right forearm, tracing a 45-degree angle between the horizontal and vertical.

Your upper arms, or biceps, are touching the sides of your chest. Your chest and shoulders are still turned back away from the ball.

"Get into the correct position coming into impact and you will be perfectly placed to deliver the club face squarely into the back of the ball."

1

2

4

5

(**picture 4**) The club, lagging behind at the start of the sequence, has now almost caught up with the hands. The club face is also almost square as the body keeps turning.

(**picture 5**) Just past impact, the club head is flush square and ready to overtake the hands.

3

(pictures 1, 2 and 3)
The start of the hand release –
the 'hammer blow' (pictures 1 and 2) –
is followed by the club face beginning
to square up to the ball (picture 3).

In an instant, the club shaft and club head
move from above the hands (picture 1) to
below them (picture 2). The key element is
an unhinging of the right wrist. In itself, it is
a small action but it initiates the all-
important hand release.

Good golfers keep their hands and wrists
live and active, not taut or tense, during the
swing. To them, this unhinging may seem
involuntary and almost imperceptible –
they may never have given it a thought.
It may feel as if it happens automatically,
as the arms swing down and centrifugal
force takes over.

However, if you have never achieved this
move before and always hold on tightly
without allowing the club shaft to release
down into the ball, then you may initially
need to feel that you are actively unhinging
your right wrist – and probably earlier in the
swing than you expect.

Many poor golfers believe that holding
onto the angle between the shaft and the
forearms is a good thing. They actively try to
keep the club head above the hands, thus
trapping it and robbing it of momentum.
They've heard of the term 'lag' and are aware
that is what professionals do. Professionals
certainly store up energy in this way – but
they also always release it, into the back of
the ball, as they come into impact.

To release your hands, and thus the club,
we repeat – the club shaft and club head
must move from above your hands to
below them as you enter the impact zone.
This is hand release.

Look at the pictures again. From the
position in picture 1 the 90-degree angle
between forearms and club shaft will
increase as the shaft accelerates. At impact,
the shaft and club head will have caught up
with the hands, forming a straight line with
the left arm.

→

1

2

4

(picture 4) ...and allowing the club to square up to the ball. There has been no independent rolling or twisting of the hands.

5

(picture 5) The textbook impact every golfer seeks. The hands have released in perfect unison with the body rotation. Look at the club face – this shot is going straight at the flag.

3

(pictures 1, 2 and 3)
The unhinging of the wrists.
The club moves from above
to level and then below the
hands, picking up speed...

The pictures on these pages show the
golfer in the same positions as on pages
22-3, although this time we are seeing
him from side on, along the (imaginary)
ball-to-target line.

Releasing your hands initiates an action
similar to a hammer blow. Imagine
hammering a nail into a piece of wood –
your forearm moves downwards, followed
by the same unhinging of the wrist to add
real snap to the blow.

Once the club starts dropping below
the hands – and only then – the right
palm, which until now has been facing
away from the golfer's body, starts to
square up and face the ball (pictures 2
and 3). You want to feel that the right
palm and the club face are perfectly
synchronised – the club face is, in effect,
an extension of the right hand (as it is
throughout the swing).

In the same way, the knuckles of the left
hand begin to square up. Notice that the
inside of the right elbow joint continues
to face forward along the path of the swing.
It does not turn around to face the ball.

But let us make something crystal clear.
This squaring up of the club face is not an
independent action. It does not happen in
isolation. It is synchronised perfectly with
your core (or belly button area) turning
through impact. The hands and club face
remain aligned with your spine.

This is the aforementioned 'body release' –
a powerful, correctly timed turn of the core,
adding mass to the strike. Hand release and
body release, carried out simultaneously,
are the signature of all good players.

Examine the pictures on pages 22-3 again.
They include two smooth, seamless arcs,
one tracking the progress of the club head
and the other of the hands as they move
through the impact zone.

We began with a position. Now we have
a movement. The club head arc, in effect,
equates to the rim of a wheel. Sense that
your club head and hands are following
these arcs. The arcs are vital. They are
your guides, your roads across the desert.
Never stray from them.

THE IMPACT ZONE – STEP 3

WHY POST-IMPACT REALLY MATTERS

It's easy to dismiss the period post-impact as irrelevant. The ball, after all, is already on its way and there is nothing the finish can do to influence its trajectory. If your finish does not look right, however, then you need to ask yourself the question: When exactly did my swing start to go wrong?

Almost always, off-balance finishes and peculiar hand or arm positions have their origins in earlier parts of the swing. They are evidence of errors that began before the ball was struck.

Ideally, your post-impact swing should provide symmetry with what has gone before. Freeze-frame your swing at any stage and each position after impact should mirror a pre-impact position.

Study these three pictures then look back at those leading into impact on pages 22-3. The hips and core continue to turn into the finish, with the core leading and providing the driving force. The left leg straightens gradually. The left knee then moves out of the way, making space for the body to turn and for the right knee to move into the space the left knee has vacated.

Having been released and accelerated, the club head, which caught up to the hands at impact, has now slightly overtaken them.

By the final picture the wrists are starting to re-hinge upwards, with the left palm, rather than the right one, now facing forwards –

1

The key point to grasp about these positions...

again, as if you were shaking someone's hand – this time standing immediately to your left. The arms are still touching the sides of the chest.

Turn over to see the same sequence side-on.

2

...is that they form a perfect mirror image...

3

...of what happens prior to impact.

→

1

2

3

(pictures 1, 2 and 3)
Just ask yourself: Do you hit these positions in your throughswing? Do your left leg and hip remain firm? Are your arms still touching your chest? And do you retain your spine and body angles? If not, then ask yourself another question: When did it all start going wrong? Probably earlier than you think.

WHERE 9 OUT OF 10 GOLFERS GO WRONG

'CLASSIC' ERRORS TO AVOID
And here's how not to do it!

This picture illustrates a classic error – the 'chicken wing' – that you will see every day, at every range and every course you visit.

Here our player has not come into the impact zone correctly. He has probably introduced hand roll (we'll examine this cardinal sin in the next chapter) at some stage of his swing – probably earlier rather than later. He is not releasing his hands, and therefore the club. Indeed, it's impossible for him to do so. And, if you don't release the club in the right way, it becomes very hard to square the face at impact and hit a straight shot.

As he approaches the ball, his left arm is bent – thus earning the 'chicken wing' tag – and his left elbow leads into impact, pointing almost down the fairway rather than into his body.

We see this position in 9 out of 10 golfers who visit us at Knightsbridge.

The club head is 'trapped' behind the hands, not overtaking them as it should. The hands can't release. The club face is open. This shot is heading way out to the right, unless our player somehow manages to flip the club face back square.

Golfers coming 'over the top' – another classic error that can look very similar to the chicken wing – start the downswing by

What not to do: The 'chicken wing' – 9 out of 10 bad golfers do this. The hands have twisted out of postion, with no unhinging of the wrists. The club head is 'trapped' and unable to accelerate through.

spinning their shoulders back towards the ball immediately, forcing the left arm away from the chest and pulling the right arm out of position as well.

Can you hit straight golf shots, playing with these methods? Yes. Occasionally. Although you'll lose out on length. And remember, good golf is about repeating constantly. Occasionally simply won't do.

BEST PRACTICE

IMPACT ZONE DRILL

We started this chapter with a set of 'frozen' positions and a list of checkpoints. Now let's swing slowly through, from the start to the end of the impact zone.

As the arms swing down, make sure you include the hand release, allowing the club face to square up to the ball. Your body will turn through. The entire movement is connected.

Make sure that you refer to the checkpoints highlighted earlier. It's essential that you get yourself in the right position before swinging down into impact. Inaccurate practice is no practice at all.

Now repeat this mini-swing, repeat it and repeat it again.

In essence, this mini-drill mimics the pros and their miniature warm-up swings. It reminds you how important the impact zone is. In fact it's not really a drill at all. It's a good habit, and a statement of intent.

Leave a few clubs around the house. Soon you'll find yourself carrying out this impact zone drill while watching TV or making toast! Carry on, until you're doing it in your sleep.

"It's essential that you get yourself in the right position before swinging down into impact. Inaccurate practice is no practice at all."

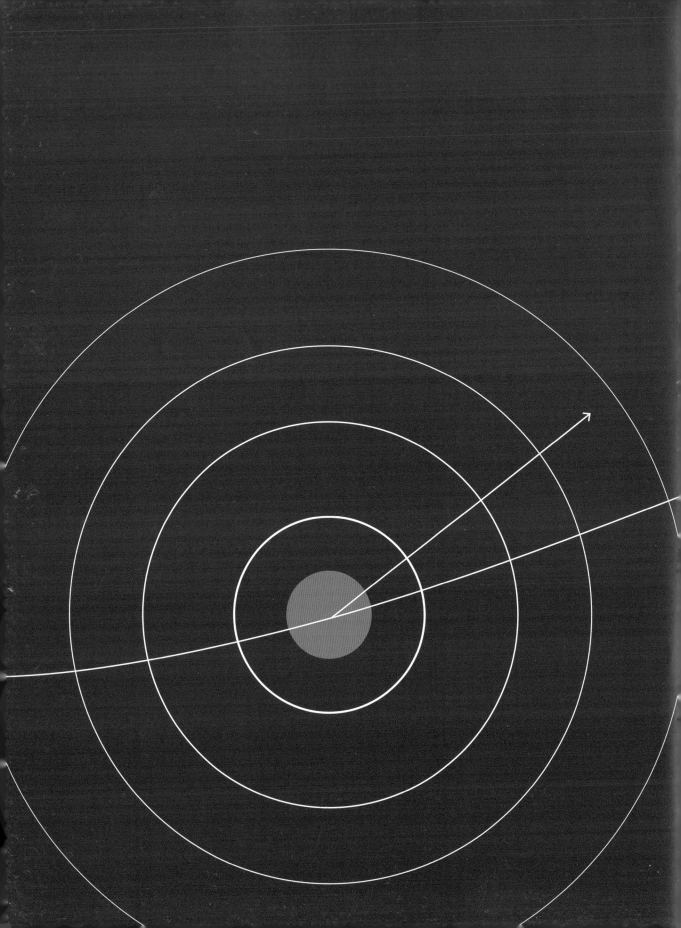

CHAPTER 2
HAND ACTION

Nothing affects the club face more
dramatically through impact than a golfer's
hand action. Most players, though, struggle
to understand how hand release and wrist
hinge – as opposed to hand roll – can
totally transform their game.

HAND ACTION

POWER WITH PRECISION

Modern golf teaching tends to concentrate on the big muscles rather than the small. It is a trend driven by today's relentless quest for power. If you want more distance, then clearly you need to think big – the big muscles in your legs, back and shoulders.

We like power and distance as well – miles of the stuff. We like big muscles too. However, there is a 'but'. What we really like is power with precision. Power precisely applied equals powerful, accurate golf shots.

This is where the small muscles – and the hands – contribute. Used correctly, they provide good golfers with both key elements – precision and power.

Your hands and wrists are as complex are they are sensitive. They're also perfectly designed for fine motor skills. Each hand is made up of 27 bones as well as scores of muscles and tendons. Your wrists are so sophisticated that they can move in almost any direction.

It follows that they can radically influence the angle of the club face.

Put another way – you'd better know how to use them if you hope to play good golf.

So, before going any further, let's take a closer look at hand action.

Firstly, let's clarify our terminology. We prefer not to use such traditional golf terms as 'pronation', 'supination' and 'dorsiflexion'. Why? Simple. Most people have no idea what they mean! We also avoid the term 'wrist cock', since it can lead to confusion.

Let's stick to 'wrist hinge' – an action we love – and 'hand roll' – one that we hate!

"What we really like is power with precision. Power precisely applied equals powerful, accurate golf shots."

WRIST HINGE

1

Imagine you are about to shake someone's hand.

2

The all-important wrist hinge, with the thumb pointing upwards.

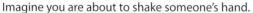

Hold your right forearm and hand horizontally, or almost horizontally, in front of you, in the middle of your chest, as if about to shake someone's hand. The top of your right bicep is touching the side of your chest – they are connected. Raise your hand a couple of inches from the wrist so that

your thumb begins to point upwards or, if the action is continued, towards your nose. This is what we call 'wrist hinge'. The elbow remains pointing down to the ground.

Do the same with your left hand held out in front of you in the middle of your chest.

1

2

Our golfer is in the same positions as opposite, but this time seen from face on. Whether done with the right or left hand, the shape at the back of the hand is retained while hinging.

The elbow stays pointing downwards and the club shaft rises vertically.

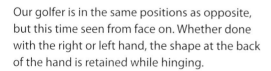

Notice the concave angle between the back of the hand and the forearm – they do not run in a perfectly straight line. This preset angle will be discussed in greater detail later. It should not be lost at any stage during the swing. Lose it and your wrist hinge will rapidly turn into hand roll.

Wrist hinge plays a crucial part in adding both speed and stability to the club shaft and club head during hand release.

HAND ROLL

Start from the same position as before.

The hand and forearm now roll in a clockwise rotation. The elbow will start to point into your side rather than straight down.

Rolling anticlockwise shows even more clearly how the elbow is pulled out of position.

THE DREADED HAND ROLL

As on page 36, hold your right forearm and hand horizontally in front of you, as if about to shake someone's hand. Turn your palm clockwise to face the ceiling, or anticlockwise to face the floor. Your forearm will turn simultaneously and your elbow may also splay in or out. This is hand roll.

Nearly all bad golfers roll their hands, particularly clockwise in the takeaway. They think this is wrist hinge. It is not. Hand (and forearm) roll has a radical and uncontrolled effect on the direction of the club face. It should play no part in a solid, repeatable golf swing.

THE CORRECT WAY TO USE YOUR HANDS

THE CLUB FACE TELLS A STORY

So what should your hands be doing as they come into the impact zone?

We believe the best way to illustrate exactly how they should work – and how that action relates to a pure golf strike – is to exaggerate the size of the club face, while also shortening the club shaft. This will underline how the hands affect the face. You could do worse than find a tennis racket – or even a frying pan – to help you understand this concept.

Begin by getting into position at the start of the impact zone, as explained in Chapter 1.

Look at the pictures opposite. By unhinging your right wrist, the club shaft and club head begin to release – they move rapidly from above the hands (picture 1) to below them (picture 2).

Note that the face of the club continues to face the same way – directly in front or away from the golfer's body – as this releasing or unhinging occurs. The face is not turning in to face the ball. If it did, you would be rolling your hands, which in turn would cause your elbows to splay.

Once the club has dropped below the hands then – and only then – is the face of the club perfectly placed to start squaring up to the ball. Again, this squaring up is not caused by the wrists rolling or flipping over. That would wreck your release. Your hands simply follow their arc as your core turns into impact (picture 3). This is what we call 'body release'.

The wrist is about to unhinge as it enters the impact zone.

The wrist, having unhinged, has now squared up to the ball, the hand and club face mirroring each other.

The hand and club face are kept square as the arms swing through impact. There is no hand roll required.

→

Unhinging the wrists while turning the body in unison will increase club shaft and club head speed into the ball – thus equating to power. These synchronised actions also ensure the club face can square up at impact – equating to precision. Seen from the front, the right arm approaches the impact zone with the wrist still hinged. By picture 2 it has unhinged, while the body has turned in unison, thus beginning to square up the club face to the ball. The arm then continues to swing down into impact, synchronised with the body rotation.

(pictures 1, 2 and 3)
The frying pan exercise, seen from the front on. This 'double move', of the arm and body, will increase club shaft and club head speed into the ball – equating to power.

1

2

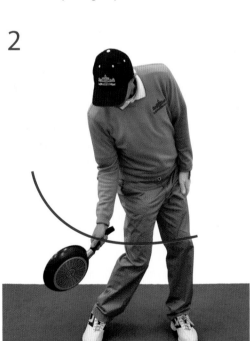

3

WHERE 9 OUT OF 10 GOLFERS GO WRONG

THE FAILURE TO RELEASE

Many weaker players, as previously stated, never release the golf club correctly. Indeed, it is actually impossible for most of them to do so. Thus they find it hard to square up their club face as they hit the ball.

Bad golf downswings come in all shapes and sizes, of course, with their owners approaching the impact zone from all angles.

But, as we said in Chapter 1, the problems encountered by 9 out of 10 golfers that we teach stem from a rolling of the hands at some stage during the swing. This leads to all sorts of trouble and they spend the rest of their time desperately – and unsuccessfully – fighting to correct these errors and get back into position before the strike.

A small minority of players, however, may approach the impact zone in the slot or on the right plane without having rolled their hands. However, most of these will still fail to release their hands because they misunderstand what they are trying to do.

The golfer pictured on this page is the same one featured in Chapter 1. He has approached the ball from a reasonable position but his failure to release his hands and thereby drop the club head from above to below them, has completely strangled his swing deep in the downswing.

He has lost all momentum, his hips have stopped turning and he has 'chicken-winged' and allowed his arms to buckle upwards.

What not to do: If you fail to release, you may end up looking like this. You've strangled your swing. You're probably going to end up shouting 'Fore right!'

He must find some way of squaring up his club face. However his chances of doing this now are minimal.

At best, this player will probably succeed in holding his club face open with firm wrists through impact, thus producing a glancing blow from left to right. Or he could roll his hands over and pull way left.

BEST PRACTICE

1

2

HAMMER IT!

A good way to master the correct hand action is to practise it directly in front of you. This will not only make it easier to see and understand wrist hinge, but it will also underline how powerful the hand release can be in delivering a hammer blow to the back of the ball.

Set up as in picture 1 above with an impact bag (you can buy these from any good golf store or, indeed, improvise by using an old holdall) directly in front of you. Bring your hands to the middle of your torso, then lift your arms up and hinge your wrists.

Swing the arms back down so that the club head strikes the bag. Do so as if you are holding a hammer. To add power, unhinge or release your wrists whilst dropping your arms. If you do not release the wrists, you will deliver a significantly less powerful blow.

This is exactly what you are trying to do in your golf swing at the start of the impact zone.

(pictures 1 and 2)
If you used a hammer or an axe, you would use wrist hinge to add power. Golf is no different.

CHAPTER 3
THE TAKEAWAY

Get the start wrong, Ben Hogan warned,
and your problems will inevitably multiply
throughout your golf swing. High-handicappers
invariably overcomplicate the takeaway.
The secret is to keep each element as simple
as possible.

THE TAKEAWAY

WHY BACK TO FRONT MAKES SENSE

Learning how to play golf by starting at impact, then working outwards, may seem like an odd way of doing things, but it makes absolute sense to us. It made absolute sense to Leslie King, the founder of the Knightsbridge Golf School, too. That is exactly how he taught his pupils. They began with miniature swings then gradually extended them.

Odd as it may sound, mastering the impact zone first makes the takeaway – normally viewed as the logical place for beginners to start – so much easier to learn.

The takeaway is defined as the start of the swing, once you have set up at address. The club head, in effect, is taken away from the ball. You'd think getting the club moving should be easy enough. Strangely, starting from a stationary position causes all sorts of problems. Why does perfecting the takeaway matter so much? Because it is a vital stage of the swing, coming a close second to the strike itself. It occurs, after all, within the all-important impact zone, where the success of each and every shot is decided. The takeaway just travels in the opposite direction, that's all.

Ben Hogan said of the first two feet of the takeaway: 'Get it wrong and the problems multiply.' In his ground breaking book *Five Lessons* he added: 'Just as one faulty movement leads to others, each correct movement makes it that much easier to execute other moves correctly.'

A large number of golfers address the ball with no idea of which part of their body should move first, nor which direction their club, hands, arms or body should take.

KNOW WHERE YOU'RE HEADING

Once you've learnt which way to return to the ball, however, the takeaway suddenly becomes much clearer. If you want to approach the ball on one line, it's logical that you should leave on this line as well. To a large extent, it's just a matter of doing the same thing in reverse.

Think of it like this – would you ever set off on a complicated journey without a map? Turn left rather than right at the first junction and you'll cause yourself problems which will last the entire trip. You might get lost immediately – many golfers do – or, alternatively, you might eventually find your way to your destination, but only after a series of complicated detours and U-turns.

Knowing where you're heading makes things so much easier.

A NATURAL MOVE

Begin by setting up at address immediately in front of a wall, without a club. Your head should almost be touching the wall.
Let your left arm hang down and tuck your right arm by your side. Concentrate solely on the way your left hand and arm move, without the distraction of watching or worrying about where the club head is going.

From this position, your arm will naturally start moving along the wall. Crucially, the left hand and wrist do not move in any other way – there is no independent hinging, twisting or rolling.

Do this correctly while adding body turn and your left hand will follow the hand arc up to the 8 o'clock position. The left arm remains in contact with the left side of the chest while maintaining the same length or radius. It does not bend at the elbow.

As the left arm initiates the first movement, so the shoulders and upper torso react, turning and drawing the left arm in.
The arm and body movements are synchronised. Different people feel different things while carrying out this movement – you may, for example, sense that the arm is going back in a straight line but that the right shoulder is turning back, thus drawing the arm inside with it.

By the end of the takeaway your hand, as seen from along the ball-to-target line, is opposite your left hip and the shoulders have turned around 45 degrees in response to the arm movement. The left shoulder has not dipped downwards.

1

Focus solely on the left arm.

Look at the final picture. Imagine the smooth hand arc extending from this position right up to the top of the backswing. It's important to know where you're heading. This arc represents the most direct route from A to B. Any other way will involve an unnecessary detour.

2

The arms swing, the shoulders react.

3

The left shoulder turns around the spine but does not dip.

STRANGE BUT TRUE

Now repeat the exercise but with both hands holding a club. Concentrate again on eliminating all independent wrist twisting or rolling. As the hands move along their arc, the club head will remain outside them, but inside the ball-to-target line. The club face, too, does not roll or twist. It follows its own arc whilst remaining square to the body.

Picture 2 provides a useful checkpoint. As you reach this stage, you'll see that the club head is roughly midway between your toes and the ball-to-target line, as well as being roughly halfway up between the level of your hands and the floor.

At this stage, the butt end of your club will be pointing at your left thigh. The club head will be below the hands.

This takeaway will feel very strange for golfers used to rolling the club head inside their hands and the ball-to-target line. It may indeed feel initially as if the club head is way in front of them and way outside the ball-to-target line. However, it won't be.

It may also feel as if there are a lot fewer moving parts, with no rolling of the wrists together with the left arm remaining straight, rather than splaying, and remaining connected to the chest. Which is just the feeling you want. A correct takeaway is deceptively simple.

1

Use a club this time, but don't let it distract you – retain the same feelings in your left hand and wrist from the previous exercise.

2

3

The midway checkpoint – halfway between the toes and the ball, halfway between the hands and the floor.

This takeaway has fewer moving parts, making it easier to master and – crucially – easier to repeat.

→

1

2

(picture 1)
The concave shape at the back of the left hand is retained.

(picture 2)
Note the inverted triangle formed by the arms and the shoulder line. This triangle also retains its shape.

(picture 3)
The movement of the arms is synchronised with the body turn.

3

KEY TAKEAWAY CHECKPOINTS

Now study the wrists from face on during the takeaway. The left hand provides a key checkpoint. At address (picture 1), you will notice there is a concave angle at the back of the left hand (as mentioned in the section on the wrist hinge in the previous chapter). This angle does not change throughout the backswing, even when the hands begin to hinge. Lose that angle and you are rolling your hands.

The club face, in effect, remains facing the ball for the first few inches of the backswing. Roll your hands clockwise and it would very quickly face away.

Notice also that the radius, or length, of the left arm has remained the same and that your head and shoulders have not dipped down (picture 2). The shoulders, arms and hands form an inverted triangular unit that maintains its shape. It does not narrow, shorten or extend, thus keeping the club head on its arc and at exactly the same distance from the golfer's core throughout the swing.

This triangle moves in synchronisation with the body turn (picture 3).

Thus the takeaway is virtually a mirror image of your entry into the impact zone during the downswing, only a little less dynamic since it is carried out more slowly.

It is imperative that you practise it slowly, meticulously and repeatedly. Practise it as far as the 8 o'clock position but no further. Practise it until it becomes your norm.

"Why does perfecting the takeaway matter so much? Because it is a vital stage of the swing, coming a close second to the strike itself. It occurs, after all, within the all-important impact zone, where the success of each and every shot is decided. The takeaway just travels in the opposite direction, that's all."

WHERE 9 OUT OF 10 GOLFERS GO WRONG

WHY MOST GOLFERS ROLL

The overwhelming majority of golfers roll their hands. Why? It's probably instinctive. They sense that the top of the backswing is somewhere over their right shoulder and feel that the quickest way to get there must be to suck the club head inside as quickly as possible.

They are mistaken.

We have strategically placed our golfer next to an imaginary wall to make the point as forcibly as possible.

The picture on the left shows the player rolling his hands, with the left arm losing its connection with the chest. His club soon strikes the wall behind him. Following this – physically, he cannot keep going in this direction – he will have to compensate by lifting the club up vertically in an attempt to complete his backswing. Expect his downswing to be equally tortuous.

In the picture on the right, meanwhile, the golfer starts by pushing his club outside the ball-to-target line, his left arm also losing contact with his chest and his club piercing the imaginary wall in front of him.

Realising he cannot continue in this direction, he will have to roll his wrists over sharply in order to bring the club back towards him. Now the club, of course, collides with the wall behind him!

Again, this backswing sets off a complicated chain of events that will corrupt the downswing, impact and beyond.

In both cases, the hands fail to follow their hand arc.

Another way of fully appreciating the correct – and incorrect – way of doing this is to focus on the butt end of the club. It serves as a useful pointer of how the hands are behaving. In the correct takeaway, the butt end continues to point inwards towards the body. Roll and twist the hands, however, and the butt end will be much more erratic. When the hands roll inside the line, for instance, the butt end will point outwards, well away from the body.

Try it.

"The takeaway is virtually a mirror image of your entry into the impact zone during the downswing, only a little less dynamic since it is carried out more slowly."

What not to do: Rolling into a wall behind you.

What not to do: Pushing into a wall in front of you.

BEST PRACTICE

LESS IS MORE

To most golfers, synchronising the arm, shoulder and torso movement in the takeaway whilst not rolling wrists or splaying elbows will seem strangely 'minimalist'.

Bad golfers tend to introduce a lot more moving parts into their swings. What we propose may feel more structured, with less going on.

We see that as a good feeling. In the takeaway, less means more.

So choke down your club – move your hands down the grip – so that the butt end presses into your core.

It should remain in exactly that position during the start of the takeaway. Roll your hands and splay your elbows, however, and the handle will immediately come away from your stomach.

Now try this exercise while facing a wall, as illustrated earlier in this chapter. Then try it with the wall directly behind you. It will quickly let you know if you are going wrong. Just use an old club (and, preferably, an old wall too).

This is an excellent way of ingraining the principle of a non-rolling takeaway – a vital building block to good golf.

"A non-rolling takeaway is a vital building block to good golf."

CHAPTER 4
THE BACKSWING

A correct backswing is the automatic reward for a correct takeaway and a correct wrist hinge. Get these right and you're perfectly set. Get them wrong, however, and your backswing will quickly go off track.

THE BACKSWING

LINKING THE TAKEAWAY AND BACKSWING
So you now know all about wrist hinge, hand release and impact – the 'business end' of the golf swing – and you also understand what to do during the takeaway. That already makes you better informed than 9 out of 10 golfers.

You are continuing to practise your miniature swing, thus avoiding the pitfalls that Hogan warned about during those all-important first few feet.

In short, you are right on track.

The next stage, however, also needs detailed attention.

Extending your swing away from the impact zone is not just a matter of turning the shoulders and lifting the arms. The link between the takeaway and the backswing also involves a gradual hinge of the wrists that does not come naturally to most players. To many, it seems counter-intuitive.

Do not be surprised, therefore, if this action does not feel comfortable. Trust us, it's correct. Drill it in by practising meticulously, in slow motion. Master it and the rest of your swing will follow seamlessly.

We ended the takeaway with the hands in the 8 o'clock position and the club head just below. Up to this point, the hands have not moved independently. They have retained the same angles they had at address. They have followed the hand arc, with the arms having initiated the movement.

Now, however, the hands begin to hinge upwards, moving the club head from below to above the hands (picture 2). Do not exaggerate this – it is a gradual rather than a sudden movement, occurring as the arms continue to lift.

To a certain extent, the start of the hinge is already preset, since your arms and club shaft, viewed from the side, form an angle at address – they do not run in a straight line down to the ground. This angle is retained up to this point in the backswing.

If this hinging action sounds familiar, well, it should. It is, in effect, the reverse of hand release as discussed in Chapters 1 and 2.

To someone used to rolling their hands, the shaft will feel unnaturally vertical as the hands hinge. You may be disconcerted by the sensation of the club head still being outside your hands i.e. slightly nearer the ball-to-target line than your hands. A 'roller' would be used to the head being flipped inwards, nearer the right leg.

This sensation, however, does not last long. As you hinge, your upper body also continues to turn over the stable lower body, while your arms begin to swing up.

This swinging up of the arms is not on a straight vertical plane (even if we did lift the club straight up in the 'Best Practice' section in Chapter 2 – this was done to keep things as simple as possible while getting the feeling of a correct hand release). The arm plane is slightly tilted, the arms

1

2

The end of the takeaway.

The gradual hinge into the backswing.

→

3

The hands move across the chest towards the right shoulder.

4

The hands reach a 'deep' position at the top, just behind the right shoulder.

swinging up from left to right as seen from the player's perspective.

Thus, viewed from the ball-to-target line in the sequence of pictures (opposite), the player's hands and arms move from in front of him, across his chest and towards the right shoulder as he nears the top.

This swinging up of the arms, synchronised with the turn of the torso – not a roll of the hands – gradually brings the club head from outside the hands, as seen at the start of the sequence, to inside them.

This must happen if your hands keep moving along their arc. If the hands, hinging gradually rather than rolling, stay on their arc, the arms will by definition be in the correct position. The hands, in effect, define where the arms go as they swing up.

Picture 2 on page 63 includes another important checkpoint. The club shaft should now run up the right forearm, or just above it. It MUST NOT drop below – or nearer to the horizontal than – the forearm. If that is the case, your hands will be rolling.

Once the hinge, synchronised with the turn of the upper body, has been correctly achieved, the rest of the backswing follows automatically. The arms come across the chest at a 45-degree angle between the horizontal and vertical, while the upper body continues to turn. The left arm remains close to the left side of the chest.

Here are some further useful checkpoints: Having hinged the club, your hands will be in line with your left hip, as seen from along the ball-to-target line (picture 2). Halfway

up, following their arc, the hands are in the middle of the chest. Three-quarters up and the hands are covering or opposite the right shoulder. At the very top, they are just behind the right shoulder – the perfect completed backswing position (picture 4).

You may sense that your arms, by swinging up, are leading this part of the backswing. Alternatively, you may feel the turn of the torso is initiating it. It does not matter, as long as both are synchronised and occurring at the same time – and as long as the hands stay on their arc. At no point does the body stop and the arms continue lifting, or vice versa. The two must work together. They arrive at the top together, and are completed at the same time as the 90-degree wrist hinge.

Do not be tempted to over hinge – that will probably only lead to hand twisting and a bending or collapsing of the arms. It is worth repeating that, apart from the upward hinge, your hand angles should be the same now as they were at address. The concave shape at the back of your left hand and forearm should still be there.

This backswing may seem oddly simple to someone used to relying on hand manipulation, elbow splaying and disconnected arms. The reason, again, is just as simple. There are fewer moving parts than you might expect.

You are now carrying out fewer movements – simple rather than complicated ones – because you have eradicated the need to compensate for earlier errors.

WHERE 9 OUT OF 10 GOLFERS GO WRONG

1

What not to do: Rolling the hands instead of hinging the wrists.

2

What not to do: Faulty wrist action leads to disconnected arms.

HOW TO WRECK A GOOD TAKEAWAY

You have to sympathise with the golfer in the first picture above. He may have mastered the takeaway, retaining his wrist angles and keeping his left arm connected to the left side of his chest, as illustrated in this chapter's first set of pictures (see page 63).

But he then finds a way of wrecking all that has gone before. Instead of hinging his wrists up, he rolls them horizontally. The action turns the club shaft over onto a flat plane and that error feeds through into the rest of his swing, dictating what follows.

His hands must now move off their arc. The club head is even further off its arc. The damage is done. His chances of returning to the 'slot' at the start of the impact zone on the downswing – and thus releasing his hands and squaring up his club into the ball – are virtually nil.

If there were a wall just behind him at this point, the club would collide with it.

In picture 2, things look just as bad. The rolling of his hands has translated directly into a faulty position at the top.

His hands are twisted and have lost their original angles, his elbows have splayed, his arms are completely disconnected from his body and the club shaft is now pointing way across the ball-to-target line, somewhere to the right of the target. In some cases, this sort of error would also cause all his weight to fall back into his left foot and left side at the top of the backswing (a position known as a 'reverse pivot').

Put simply, the golf swing is a chain reaction. A faulty wrist action may feel minor and innocuous but it provokes another faulty position, followed by yet another. Ultimately, rolling wrists disconnect the arms, then the club head, from the body including the vital core area.

A talented player may somehow find his way back to the ball through a series of compensations. For lesser players, however, it is already too late. They will have to rely on Lady Luck to hit a straight shot from here.

Before we complete our study of the backswing, let us consider what Jack Nicklaus said about hinging the wrists.

For him, it felt as if the weight and the fluid movement of the club hinged his wrists for him. He sensed there was a gradual 'loading' of the wrists as the backswing progressed. He called it 'reactive' hinging.

We like what Nicklaus says. Some people may share this feeling of the hands continuing to hinge in a gradual, smooth action all the way up the top of the backswing. At any one point in the swing, the hinge movement is so infinitesimal that it's hard to spot. It happens throughout.

Others may feel the hinge as a definite move, occurring at a particular point.

Both methods, though, carried out correctly, should end with a 90-degree wrist hinge.

For poor players and learners, though, a dramatic early hinge of the wrists can cause problems, tensing the muscles in the forearms and causing the arms to bend up as well. They will thus shorten and lose their width or radius as measured from the middle of the chest.

As shown in the picture on the right, an excessive, early hinge causes the left arm to break at the elbow, causing a loss of radius or width which will have to be rectified somewhere later in the swing.

Some players may also lose posture by dipping down towards the ball as they pick up the club rather than letting it swing away from them. Their weight may also fall across to the left rather than rotating to the right.

A FAULT REQUIRES A CORRECTION

Again, these golfers will require a secondary move later in their swing to try and get back to their full 'address' height by the time they approach impact.

A fault thus requires a correction just to get back to the status quo, making the swing much more complicated – and harder to repeat – than it needs to be.

What not to do: An early, excessive wrist hinge can lead to a loss of radius as the left arm breaks at the elbow.

BEST PRACTICE – PART I

1

2

Address the ball, then lift your arms and hinge your wrists until the shaft is horizontal.

Turn your upper body to the right – the movement is slightly exaggerated in the image above. Do not change your overall posture.

3

Turn your feet and lower body to face the club.

A DRILL FIT FOR A KING

The following exercise, based on one used by Leslie King, is simple to perform, yet may put you in a position you have never experienced before – the perfect halfway back position. It's so simple, indeed, that you may wonder why you've never managed it

before. The answer – and we don't apologise for the repetition – is that you've probably been rolling your hands.

Address the ball, then lift your arms and hinge your wrists slightly so that the club shaft is horizontal to the ground (picture1). Maintaining your posture, turn your shoulders around 90 degrees to the right (picture 2). Keep your head level – it may be tempting to stand up as you turn, but resist – while also keeping your left arm touching the left side of your chest.

Without perhaps realising it, you are now in a perfect position, halfway through your backswing. Notice the preset concave shape at the back of your left hand has not changed from address – there has been no independent hand movement apart from the small upward hinge – nor has the forearm rolled or the left arm worked away from the left side of the chest.

To complete the exercise, turn your lower body and feet round to face the club again (picture 3). Hey presto! You're back where you started – apart, of course, from having turned your body 90 degrees to the right. Crucially, you hands have retained the same shape, while your arms and torso, connected together, have moved as one unit.

When you think you've mastered this exercise, get a friend or, even better, a teacher, to check it. Then do it again. And again. And again. You may get dizzy, it's true. But you'll also start ingraining a key position that must form part of your backswing.

BEST PRACTICE – PART II

A LESSON IN UNDERSTANDING

This is not so much a physical exercise as an exercise in understanding – in understanding, that is, what the left arm is doing during the backswing. Some people struggle to understand what we mean when we talk of swinging the left arm up on a 45 degree angle. If so, this should help clarify the issue.

Stand upright, holding your club in your left hand and hanging your left arm down by the left side of your body, near your pocket. Feel free to move your hand further down the grip than normal so that your arm is full extended by your side. Now swing your arm up towards your right shoulder, while retaining the angle in your left hand and not rolling it.

There you have it – that is exactly what you do in the golf swing. Your arm has lifted on a 45-degree angle, and it will be matched by the angle of the club shaft. All that is required to complete the action – and your backwing – is to add a turn of the shoulders.

Another way to think of this is to focus on the hand moving up its arc. This should produce exactly the same result.

The alternative would be to swing your arm straight up vertically, or around horizontally. The first option would produce a backswing on a very high plane, while the other result would be very flat.

Try these positions, adding in some shoulder turn – then try to work out how you would get back to the ball! It does not take a genius to see that neither method is conducive to getting the arms and the body to work together in the downswing.

VIRTUOUS CIRCLES, VICIOUS CIRCLES

Golfers with vertical-plane swings often rely more on their arms to try to generate power in the downswing. They are prone to coming over the top and slicing.

Players with flat swings, meanwhile, miss out on the power provided by the swing of their arms. Approaching the ball horizontally and from the inside, they tend to push the ball or, if they flip their hands over, hook it low and left.

Realising this, they will try to solve the problem by rolling their wrists or pulling their hands off the hand arc in an attempt to somehow present a square club face to the ball.

What they are really doing, though, is overlaying one error over another.

Far easier to avoid the initial error and thus avoid the need to compensate. Far easier to understand, in this case, what your left arm should be doing in the first place. Getting the basics right leads to a virtuous circle. Getting them wrong starts a vicious one.

CHAPTER 5

THE BACKSWING: MORE DETAIL, LESS JARGON

Backswing faults often have exotic names, like the 'flying right elbow'. Most errors, though, require simple rather than exotic remedies. Here are the common errors to watch out for, along with the best ways to correct and avoid them.

THE BACKSWING: MORE DETAIL, LESS JARGON

PRECISION AND PURPOSE
You might already have noticed that we are very keen on detail!

A lot of golf instruction isn't so detail-orientated, preferring instead to paint in broad brushstrokes. Why? Because it's easier. In some cases, it even camouflages a lack of understanding (a lot of fine golfers, indeed, can't clearly explain what they are doing – they just do it).

It's certainly easier to discuss things in generalities. But all that does is leave students with even more questions, for example, 'What exactly do you mean by that?'

Generalities don't work in golf. It's no good, after all, hitting the ball in the 'general' direction of the flag.

And it's no good 'generally' hoping to improve either. Getting better at the game takes precision and purpose.

Jargon often doesn't work either. It should be a short cut, a concise way of expressing something complicated. But both speaker and listener must understand exactly what the jargon stands for. If they don't, it's self-defeating – a short cut up a blind alley.

So, as we head for the top of the backswing, let's tackle a few common queries – for example the 'flying elbow' and 'the concave/convex left wrist'. After demystifying the jargon first, of course.

"Generalities don't work in golf. It's no good, after all, hitting the ball in the 'general' direction of the flag."

THE RIGHT ELBOW

A picture-postcard backswing.

A 'flying elbow' pulls the arm 'triangle' out of shape.

MAKE YOUR BACKSWING A NO-FLY ZONE

The 'flying elbow' refers to an incorrect fold or bend of the right arm as it approaches the top of the backswing.

Study the pictures opposite.

In the first picture our golfer has completed a perfect backswing. The torso has turned, the left arm has remained connected to the chest and retained its radius (or length) while lifting on its 45-degree angle across the chest. The hands have retained their angles, with the slight 'cup' or concave shape at the back of the left hand exactly as it was at address. There has been no hand manipulation. Everything has stayed connected.

The right elbow, meanwhile, has folded upwards, forming a 90-degree angle between bicep and forearm, while the angle of that forearm, seen from along the ball-to-target line, is pretty much parallel to the spine angle. Again, nothing has changed. The fundamental angles of the right arm – which, of course, has folded upwards – are the same as they were at the start.

How can you check this? Stand with a mirror facing your right shoulder along the ball-to-target line. Without using a club, go from address to the top of your backswing. Now, without moving your body, simply let your right arm unfold and hang down to your right side. Look into the mirror – the shape of your right arm (and hand) will be just as it was seen from face-on at address.

Another useful checkpoint is the inverted triangle formed by the arms and shoulders. As you lift your arms in the backswing, the shape of this triangle barely changes (even though it folds up on itself). The distance between the forearms remains the same as the right elbow folds up (it might increase by one or two finger-widths, but no more), while the elbows are level with each other.

The second picture shows a different scene.

Here, the right arm has folded out on an angle. The elbow is now pointing behind the golfer's back rather than downwards. The right forearm is not parallel to the spine but now nearer to horizontal.

That, in turn, has affected the position of the left arm, the width and length of the inverted triangle (pulled out of shape, it is now wider and shorter), the shape of the hands and the line of the club shaft, which is now pointing across the ball-to-target line. All the angles have changed… and all will have to be changed back again during the downswing.

Yes, it is possible to play very good golf with a 'flying elbow'. But it introduces a series of complications that you could well do without.

WRIST CUPPING AND CLUB FACE ANGLES

The wrists and arms retain precisely the same shape and relationship they shared at address – and the club face stays square.

Twisting the wrists into a cupped shape opens the club face. This invites a sliced shot.

Rolling the wrists into a bowed shape shuts the club face. This one is inviting a low hook.

KEEPING IT SIMPLE

A lot of players worry about the shape of the left wrist at the top of the backswing. Should the wrist and forearm be flat? Should there be a cup at the back of the hand? And what effect does all this have on the club face?

For us, it's very simple.

If you start with a good grip and don't roll your wrists or forearms, if your takeaway is textbook and your hands continue along the hand arc during the backswing, you can't help but get things right at the top.

As picture 1 illustrates, there will be a small cup at the back of the left hand – just as there was at address – and the leading edge of the club face will match the angle of your left forearm.

Picture 2, in contrast, depicts a much bigger cupping, thus leaving an open club face, its leading edge almost vertical. This manipulation of the wrist invites a slice.

Picture 3 shows the opposite extreme, the hand having bowed and completely lost its cup. It is now in a convex position, compared to a concave position in picture 2. The leading edge of the club face is now shut, or near horizontal. It invites a low hook.

Will you see some top players in this position? Yes, a minority of them. They will introduce extra compensation in the downswing to fix things. They have the ability to do this. You probably don't.

THE FAKE BACKSWING

(top left and top right)
The body rotates, the arms swing up, the wrists keep their shape – what could go wrong?

(bottom left and bottom right)
The body slides and tilts, the arms collapse, the wrists twist – what could go right?

THE REAL DEAL

Let's conclude with something which, in contrast to the previous two subjects in this chapter, is rarely discussed – the 'fake backswing'.

Why? Because most people don't even know they do it, let alone that it exists.

A full backswing involves a 90-degree shoulder turn over a 45-degree turn of the hips. This rotation – as opposed to lateral swaying – is compact, balanced and full of potential. The backswing also involves keeping your left arm straight – or very nearly straight – retaining the inverted triangular shape of your arms (despite some upward folding of the elbows) and not rolling your wrists.

Many golfers, though, take the easy way out. As they set up the ball, they know roughly where they want their hands and club to end up – somewhere over their right shoulder, right? Well, the easiest way to get there is to roll the wrists and bend the arms, collapsing them near the back of the neck. That way, you don't need to turn much. Perfect.

Or perhaps not.

The pictures opposite should speak for themselves. One is a real golfer. The other is an impersonator.

Just look at the amount of rotation of the shoulders and hips in the two examples. Examine the golfers' weight and balance, viewed from face on.

You will see that the body shapes of these two golfers are completely different (we will return to the way that the body should move during the backswing in the next chapter).

Consider the arms, and the triangle of the arms as viewed from the ball-to-target line. Look at the radius, and see how far the hands are from each player's chest. One has stayed on the hand arc, one has dropped short and slipped within it.

Study the hands in relation to the right shoulder – one player has turned fully, the other has under-turned, thus undermining his downswing. Look at the wrists and the angle at the back of the left hand.

One of these golfers is the real deal. The other is a fake.

CHAPTER 6
THE BIGGER PICTURE

Attention to detail is everything in the
golf swing, but it must be married with
an appreciation of the bigger picture.
The hands and arms depend on a body
that rotates, rather than slides, and retains
good angles throughout the swing.

THE BIGGER PICTURE

1

2

4

5

3

(pictures 1–5)
Perfecting the golf swing can mean focusing on many different, highly detailed elements. But never forget the bigger picture – the body turns, the arms swing, the hands follow their arc.

We've got this far without mentioning such basics as grip, posture or alignment, let alone ball position or pre-shot routines. For us, these fundamentals have been adequately covered in virtually every golf instruction book ever written (although we do refer to these issues in our appendix).

We prefer to home in on the impact zone, hand release, the hand arc and those key elements of the swing that we believe have not been adequately explained, let alone understood.

It is still important, however, to consider the bigger picture, the bigger muscles and how the body moves in conjunction with a detailed arm swing and correct hand action.

Again, your best ally will be the pictures (opposite and above) – as well as your full-length mirror.

Take your stance at address, your right shoulder will settle comfortably below the left (picture 1). Note the concave angle at the back of the left wrist – this shape should be retained throughout the swing.

The arms, alive and active as they hang down, and the hands initiate the takeaway. The hands, by following the hand arc, effectively determine where the arms go. The arms swing freely and naturally. The shoulders react by rotating around the spine.

The left shoulder may seem to drop just a fraction as it starts to move but it is merely rotating around the spine. An appreciable early drop of the left shoulder would provoke a damaging 'tilt', not a rotation, which would lead to the left side collapsing and the right side rising.

THINK 'TURN', THINK 'SPINE'

Note in pictures 1 and 2 on page 86 how the left arm is straight, though not rigid. It maintains the radius of the swing. The inside of the right elbow is visible and faces forwards, with the elbow facing back at the hip, before it begins to fold.

Crucially, there has been no swaying of the hips, upper body or head away from the target (see pictures 3 and 4 on pages 86-7). The shoulders and torso turn over a flexed right knee and over the right hip, with the weight remaining on the inside, not the outside, of the right foot. (To experience this sensation, wedge a golf ball under the outside of the right foot; this will stop your right leg from bracing or straightening.)

Lesser players, having heard that they should transfer their weight during the backswing, tend to push their left shoulder – and their entire weight – over their right foot. This can provoke a lateral movement, shifting the spine across towards the right foot and taking the head with it, while impeding the turn. Better players, in contrast, may sense their right side turning and clearing behind them, causing a pure body rotation with minimal lateral movement. The body is turning, not rocking sideways.

As the arms swing up, the body stays down. The right hip remains at the same height throughout – thanks to the right knee staying flexed – as does the golfer's head. The shoulders complete a 90-degree shoulder turn, the left shoulder touching the chin, while the hips turn around 45 degrees.

The wrists have hinged gradually throughout the backswing, reaching a 90-degree hinge at the top.

"It's not difficult to recognise a good address position. There's the comfortably straight back, the bend from the hips and the slight knee flex. There's no crouching, stiffness or slumping."

1

2

4

5

3

It's not difficult to recognise a good address position. The comfortably straight back, the bend from the hips and the slight knee flex. As Leslie King said, it looks 'balanced and poised, neither sloppy nor taut'. There's no crouching, stiffness nor slumping.

The arms hang down, around a fist's width away from the front of the thighs (a little more for longer clubs like the driver). Note the preset angle between the arms and shaft (picture 1) – the same angle can be seen from face-on as the club reaches waist height in the backswing, just as the wrists begin to hinge.

During the takeaway, the hands do not roll. The left arm remains connected to the left side of the chest. By the end, the hands are in line with the left hip, the cup in the back of the left hand is still intact and the shoulders, responding to the arm movement, have turned around 45 degrees.

(pictures 1–5)
The most striking thing about this sequence is the simplicity and sharpness of the movements. They're clean, there is no hand rolling, arm splaying, tilting or lateral swaying. Each extraneous movement requires a compensation to try to deal with the initial fault. Here, less adds up to more.

From this angle too, you can see that the left shoulder has not dipped.

Similarly, the right knee remains flexed throughout – it barely moves, in fact – while the right hip stays at the same height. There is no 'standing up' or rising of the spine angle either – the shoulders simply rotate around it. The body stays down, the arms move up.

All these movements allow the hands to follow their arc and position the club shaft along the right forearm (or just above it, as shown in picture 3, but never below it). As the arms lift, they cross the chest at a 45-degree angle. This is synchronised with the continuing body turn. Look how the right hip has moved back and around to facilitate the rotation.

By the top of the backswing, the shoulders have turned 90 degrees from their starting position and the hips 45 degrees. The right forearm, having folded upwards, is parallel to the spine and the left arm is opposite the right shoulder. The hands are above and just behind the right shoulder.

There is another angle to consider – the line across the top of the shoulders bisects the spine at 90 degrees (as seen in pictures 4 and 5). The spine angle has remained the same – as has the level of the head – despite the rotation and lifting of the arms. There is no 'standing up' in the backswing. Maintaining a constant height is crucial.

WHERE 9 OUT OF 10 GOLFERS GO WRONG

THE DREADED REVERSE 'PIVOT' – AND HOW TO AVOID IT

The previous pictures in this chapter illustrate how to perform the perfect backswing. Keep faithful to the checkpoints and you will be able to emulate it. Ignore the checkpoints and you'll fall into a series of common traps.

The hands, arms and body move together in a synchronised fashion in a good golf swing. Turn your body in the wrong way, however, and it will not allow the arms to swing freely. That, in turn, will affect the hands, causing them to lose their angles and fail to release the club correctly.

There are, of course, thousands of ways to perform a bad golf swing. We only have room for one example here. It's an example, however, that you'll often see. There's even a name for it – the 'reverse pivot'.

Our poor player, to put it bluntly, has got himself into a real mess. As is so often the case, his problems began very early in the backswing.

By tilting and dropping his left shoulder and straightening his right knee, he has blocked the free swing of his arms, as well as blocking his ability to rotate his body. His torso, spine and head have tilted back over his left foot.

To hit the ball from this position, he will have to carry out a series of highly complex movements during the downswing in order to reverse this tilt at high speed.

Wish him luck.

What not to do: The shoulders tilt and the right knee straightens in the backswing. The body isn't rotating and the arms are stuck.

Finally, look at the shape of his body at the top of his backswing, then compare it with our textbook golfer. The lesser golfer's right side is vertically straight and leaning back towards the target. The good golfer's right side, meanwhile, is indented at the waist.

He has turned. He's playing golf.
His poor relation has tilted and swayed.
He's muddling through.

BEST PRACTICE

How to do it: This player is rotating around his spine, his right side turning away behind him and his right knee remaining flexed. His arms are free to swing.

For this drill, let's take our minds off some of the detail of the previous chapters and concentrate on the way the body moves.

Set up at address, bending forward from the hips. Place a club along your toe line as a reference point. Now place a second club across it, bisecting it at a 90-degree angle, where the ball would be (in the middle of your stance, or slightly nearer the left foot). Hold a third club across your shoulders and parallel to the ground, with the butt end protruding beyond your left side and the club head beyond your right side.

Turn into your backswing until the butt end of the club held across your shoulders points down towards the second club – where the ball would be. Do not allow your spine angle to change by standing up or by swaying away from the ball.

Now turn through impact, continuing until the other end of the club across your shoulders points at the second club. Do this and you will have completed a tight and efficient rotation of the torso.

If you sway laterally and tilt rather than rotate your shoulders around your spine, the end of the club placed across your shoulders will never point at the second club, either when you turn back or through. Similarly, this will not happen if you stand up and lose your posture during the swing.

This may seem like little more than a warm-up drill but it will also let you know immediately whether or not you are rotating your body correctly.

CHAPTER 7
THE TRANSITION

The transition is the slowest part of the swing. As such, it should surely be the easiest to perform. Giving oneself time and room during the change from backswing to downswing, however, is something that players must learn.

THE TRANSITION

SMOOTHLY DOES IT

There seems to be a lot of confusion about the transition in the golf swing. 'Is it part of the backswing?' people ask. 'Or part of the downswing?' 'Or is it an independent entity in itself?'

'Should there be a pause at the top? And is it really possible for your arms to be going in one direction while your legs go in the other?'

Let's keep things simple.

The hands, arms and body all reach the top of the backswing in sync, then start coming back down together. As the arms reach the top and change direction they slow right down. The transition is the slowest part of the golf swing – slower even than the takeaway.

Having mastered the backswing, all you need to do is return down the same path that you came up on. It's that straightforward. Perfect your hand arc during the backswing, then reverse the action. Don't rush.

(It is true that, for some players, the club shaft naturally returns towards the ball on a slightly shallower plane during the downswing. That's fine. But it's not something you need to think about.)

Think hand arc, think time and think room – give yourself time and room as you start back towards the ball. Very few high-handicappers manage this.

It will help to think of the transition as a sharp bend in the road. Rush into it and you'll skid wildly off the track. Slow down into the bend and you'll not only keep on line, but there'll also be plenty of time to accelerate out of it.

As with the impact zone, a good transition is all about finding the right slot. Most high-handicappers go up on one plane only to hurtle back down on a very different one in their attempt to get from 0–100mph instantaneously.

No wonder there are so many car crashes out there.

Let's go for action rather than words to illustrate what we mean.

"As with the impact zone, a good transition is all about finding the right slot."

BEST PRACTICE

1

Set up as usual...

2

...swing to the top...

THE SLOW-MO SWING (BUT ULTRA SLOW-MO IS EVEN BETTER)

Take your address position (picture 1), then swing to the top (picture 2). As you approach it, focus on your hand arc. Your hands should be opposite the right shoulder, then just behind it at the very top.

Now, concentrating on your arms, swing them down freely on the same arc to around chest height – the end of the transition (picture 3). Keep your shoulders fully turned back as you do this. Swing in slow motion or, even better, ultra slow motion. Do not feel that you are pulling down with your arms, just let them swing (it used to be taught – wrongly – that you should tug your arms down in the same way that you would pull on a bell rope).

Now go back to the top again (picture 4). Repeat this 'pumping' movement up and

3

...swing the arms down to around chest height...

4

...before going back to the top again. Keep repeating the last two stages before swinging down and through to the finish.

down, keeping your arms alive and active rather than tensing them, with the left one straight and naturally extended. Make the movement as slow as you can. And keep sensing and feeling the hand arc, as if it were a physical rail with your hands attached to it.

Bank these feelings – especially if they don't feel like anything you've experienced before. Finally, swing through to the finish at normal speed.

THE BUMP

knee moves
across

downward
pressure

At the top of the backswing and with most of the player's weight having moved into his right side, the arms begin to drop down just as...

...the left foot, knee and hip reset themselves by bumping back across towards the target.

SYNCHRONISING ARMS AND BODY

So the transition – the end of the backswing and the start of the downswing – involves nothing else than an independent lifting and dropping of the arms while keeping the hands on the hand arc?

Well, yes… and no.

Let's stress that the previous exercise (pages 98-9), while a simplification, is very valuable. So many players have a faulty, over-vigorous body action preventing their arms from swinging back down correctly. For them, simply pumping the club up to the top and down again is the perfect way of focusing on their arms and learning how to free them. It's a key step in 'grooving' the correct hand arc and arm action.

In reality, swinging the arms down does not happen in isolation. It is synchronised with a micro-movement by the left side of the body. As the arms go through the transition, the left side resets itself by bumping back across towards the target while pressure is pushed back down into the ground through the left foot, knee, then hip and pelvis. The left knee, which may have kinked in and away from the target on the backswing, returns to the position it was at address.

Some people refer to this as weight shift, others as a small lateral 'bump'. Whatever you call it and however you feel it, it's certainly hard to spot with the naked eye. The movement used to be much easier to identify back in the days of Nicklaus and Co.

Then, players would lift their left heel in the backswing. The heel would then come back down to the ground as the left leg and side reset itself.

Imagine skimming a stone. It's the same action. There, too, you reset your weight into your left side as you prepare to throw.

Some golfers will tell you that they feel their arms are still moving backwards towards the top as their left foot, knee, leg and hip start to move forwards towards the target. It's a valid point. Very few golfers, after all, come to a complete stop at the top of the backswing. At this stage, though, we feel this could be over complicating the issue.

We prefer a simpler explanation.

We've used colour in the illustrations opposite to highlight the pressure or weight returning to the left foot and left side as the arms begin the downswing. It might help to imagine a link running through your body between the left hand and the left foot. They move simultaneously.

We would like to add a further detail. As the arms swing down, the shoulders also move a whisker. It probably feels as if they don't, but they do begin to turn towards the target. Since they're connected to the arms, they have to move with them. But again, this is a very small, barely discernible movement. It appears, indeed, that the shoulders remain fully turned as the arms drop.

WHERE 9 OUT OF 10 GOLFERS GO (WENT!) WRONG

You may have noticed that we have slightly amended our heading for this section. The reason is simple. Most poor golfers went wrong long before reaching this point of the swing.

Their errors, often dating back to the takeaway, have accumulated and compounded themselves during the backswing. These players may have rolled their wrists, let their hands come off the hand arc, lost radius by collapsing their arms or swayed rather than turned. Some of them, indeed, may have perpetrated all of these crimes!

By now, they could be in almost any position.

The best advice at this stage – although it is advice that most high-handicappers refuse point-blank to heed (which is why they remain high-handicappers) – would be to throw away this swing, go back to Chapter 1 and start correcting things from the very start.

Otherwise, it's like trying to fix a compound fracture with a sticking plaster.

Players who have rolled their hands inside and on a flat plane will have to add a loop to try and get back into position. Others, having lifted their arms too vertically, may pull them back in while trying to move their body out of the way. Players with 'fake' backswings will also desperately be trying to get out of their own way.

Let's face it – if your hands did not find the ideal position or 'slot' at the top (just behind the right shoulder as seen from the ball-to-target line), and if you don't allow your hands and arms to swing back down so that they can return on the 45-degree line, then you are likely to be in trouble.

Good players, it is often said, seem to find plenty of time and room coming down.

As we've stressed above, lesser players run out of room. The more their space is squeezed the more tangled their swings become.

Time is also an issue.

High handicappers often give in to the instinct of rushing back towards the ball as quickly as possible. It's almost a reflex. As we've said before, their attempts to get from 0–100mph instantaneously are doomed to fail. They engage the wrong muscle groups and move the wrong parts of the body as they fling themselves back round towards the ball. All thoughts of connection, hand arc, radius and release lost in the resulting blur.

A golf swing without structure is no golf swing at all. Ultimately, poor golfers end up with no time and no room to hit the ball correctly. Sometimes, indeed, it seems miraculous that they make contact at all.

Remember, if you are one of these players – good things come to those who wait.

CHAPTER 8
THE DOWNSWING

The downswing provides a seamless link between the top of the backswing and the all-important impact zone. The hands swing down on virtually the same arc that they followed on the way up. It's easy to perfect if you know where you've come from – and where you're headed.

THE DOWNSWING

THE IDEAL PATH

For anyone who has perfected the transition and the impact zone, this chapter will be a formality. The downswing? It's simply the bit in between, seamlessly blending the two together.

Having bumped your weight across, centred your body and allowed your arms to drop down to shoulder height, you're ideally set. You already know exactly where you want to be as you enter the impact zone. Now it's just a matter of going from A to B.

Or, to put it another way, it's just a matter of following the hand arc down on the path that will allow your hands to release and execute a perfect delivery into the ball.

Get your hands in the correct position and the club head will, by definition, be in the right place as well. The hand arc defines the club head arc.

Most golfers fail to follow this ideal path. Having lost their way, their only hope of making contact with the ball is to adjust their body and twist or roll their hands in compensation. Gifted players can get away with it – for a while at least. For the rest, it means a mishit rather than a square, flush contact.

1

The hands are in a 'deep' position behind the right shoulder – touching an 'imaginary' wall.

2

The hands have dropped. The shoulders look like they have not rotated back towards the ball (although, in reality, they have).

FOLLOWING THE HAND ARC

Let's examine the key checkpoints as you start the downswing.

Seen from along the ball-to-target line, your arms still form an inverted triangle, the left one straight and the right one folded at the elbow. The left arm swings down on the same 45-degree angle across your chest that it rose up on. The right arm unfolds gradually as it falls.

For golfers prone to spinning their shoulders round towards the ball too early in the downswing, this will feel as if the arms are dropping straight down and into a very 'deep' position behind them. If there were a wall directly behind them, they would sense their hands almost brushing down it during the start of the downswing (see picture 1 and 2).

We must emphasise, though, that this feeling is caused by what they *used* to do. In reality, their hands would drop vertically only for a matter of inches, if at all, before joining the 45-degree line.

From this ball-to-target line viewpoint, it looks as if the shoulders have not turned

3

The hands are in this position opposite the middle of the chest but they will feel very 'deep' for players used to spinning their shoulders over the top.

4

The shaft comes down on the 45-degree line.

at all as the arms begin to drop. Seen from the front, though (pages 110-11), the left shoulder has clearly shifted a fraction away from the chin. It has to. Despite what it feels or looks like, the arms and body are synchronised. Both are moving in unison – it's just that the arm drop is more pronounced than the shoulder turn.

The descending club shaft, again seen from along the ball-to-target line, also describes a 45-degree angle between the horizontal and vertical. It stays on this angle as it swings down, running through the tip of the right shoulder or just below it (see

picture 3). As your arms continue to fall and your body continues to turn, you will already be anticipating the impact zone and the subsequent hand release.

Halfway down, your hips will be square to the ball-to-target line, as they were at address and your shoulders will look as if they have remained fully turned. Approaching the impact zone, your hips will be beginning to open out towards the target (they will be around 45 degrees open at impact) while your shoulders will still be facing behind the ball, with about a third of their turn still to go.

1

As the arms drop and the weight shifts back across towards the left foot…

2

…the left shoulder starts to rotate, losing contact with the chin.

Viewing the pictures from pages 108-9 face on (above), notice how the golfer remains inside imaginary lines or walls running vertically down from his shoulders. Having bumped across and recentred himself during the transition (see picture 2), the knees and body look similar to their position at address. There is no violent lateral movement of the lower body. It supports the rotating upper body rather than sliding across towards the target.

A big slide and a driving of the legs were key features of golf theory until Leadbetter and Faldo teamed up in the 1980s.

They will hinder the swinging of the arms – and probably give you backache, too. The left arm retains the radius of the swing, as measured from the sternum. It has not shortened. This is clear throughout the entire picture sequence above

Meanwhile the 90-degree hinge between the left forearm and the club shaft is retained as the arms head towards the impact zone. The right palm mirrors the club face halfway down. Both face directly in front of the golfer and away from his body, rather than being turned over towards the ball by a rolling of the hands.

3

The body is recentred after bumping back across, but there is no big lateral slide.

4

The right hand faces forward as the arms fall. The hands are following the hand arc.

The hands do not twist or roll as they follow their arc downwards.

Picture the hand arc, as depicted in red in the pictures above. Imagine it as a physical, circular rail that your hands are attached to and have to follow. Retain this mental image while ensuring that your hands follow it throughout the swing.

WHERE 9 OUT OF 10 GOLFERS GO WRONG

FROM A TO B

Again, as in the previous chapter, if you are way off line or out of position in your downswing the best advice we can give is to go back to the beginning to find out where things started to go wrong.

The average downswing lasts less than half a second. For normal golfers, that's simply not enough time to salvage a miracle shot from the wreckage.

Some highly gifted players do somehow manage it. But they are hardly a model for the rest of us.

To be fair, many average golfers do learn to drop their arms on a good plane, back down the line that they came up on. Many of them look pretty good during the downswing. They seamlessly link the slot at the top with the slot at the start of the impact zone. For them, the problem centres around their inability to release the club, something we focus on in the next chapter.

Others never get it right, unable to retain the image of the hand arc on the way down and unable to curb their instinct to rush back down at the ball.

Take the player who comes 'over the top'. He has initiated his downswing by spinning his shoulders round, leaving his lower body behind. This move immediately throws the hands, arms and club shaft outside the ball-to-target line.

What not to do: The arms are disconnected and the left arm is 'chicken-winging', thus blocking the hand release.

Thus out of position and with his arms totally disconnected from his torso, he compensates by pulling his arms round at the ball (see picture above). There is no synchronised dropping of the arms and turning of the body, since they are no longer working in unison.

Whatever. Missing the slot, or the entrance to the impact zone, is golfing suicide. This swing is leaking power throughout the downswing and slowing down just when it should be speeding up.

BEST PRACTICE

FROM SLOT TO SLOT

Let's take a step back and refer to the practice drill in the previous chapter.

Then, we swung down from the top in ultra slow motion, the hands following the hand arc until they reached chest height, before pumping the arms back to the top. The key point was to sense the hand arc as if it actually existed and to use it as a guide.

Do the same again, only continue swinging the arms down until they reach the start of the impact zone, with the wrists about to release.

Imagine there is a 'slot' for your hands to fit into, at the top of the backswing and just behind your right shoulder. Similarly, imagine there is a 'slot' waiting for your hands as they enter the impact zone. This is the same position we described right at the start of Chapter 1.

It's now just a matter of passing through those two slots, linking them seamlessly together while respecting the various checkpoints listed earlier in this chapter. Again, slow motion is best. As you get used to these new feelings, they will progressively turn into automatic reflexes – or 'muscle memory'.

"The average downswing lasts less than half a second. For normal golfers, that's simply not enough time to salvage a miracle shot from the wreckage. Some highly gifted players do manage it. But they are hardly a model for the rest of us."

CHAPTER 9
THE GOLDEN RULE

The impact zone defines both the direction
of the shot as well as the quality of the
strike. A pure strike can be heard and felt.
True compression is key to great ball
striking. Many golfers, however, never
master this skill.

THE GOLDEN RULE

THE BIT THAT MATTERS MOST

So here we are, back at The Golden Rule. Back at the impact zone. Back at the bit that matters most.

As we said right at the outset, if you want to play great golf you'll need a textbook impact zone. You can't fudge it. You can't approximate it.

And, of course – to return to our road-trip analogy – knowing exactly where you've been heading will have made all the difference to the rest of your swing up to this point.

The impact zone is where you've been heading. You've just completed your downswing. You're anticipating what comes next. Your hands have followed their downward arc, in preparation for a pure strike. We're back where we began.

A FAMILIAR POSITION

Do these pictures look familiar? They should, and so too should the following text. And hopefully the positions they depict are starting to feel comfortably familiar as well.

Here's a quick recap. Your chest and shoulders are still facing behind the ball, while your core and hips have turned back to square (or even a fraction beyond square) to the ball-to-target line. Your body is balanced and centred, not sliding laterally. Your arms, naturally extended, have plenty of space in which to swing.

Your hands are just below hip height – at 8 o'clock on an imaginary clock face – with your right palm facing to the front and away from your body, mirroring the club face.

Your wrists are hinged, forming a 90-degree angle between forearms and club shaft. Your right elbow is pointing towards your right hip, with the inside of the joint facing in front.

Seen from along the ball-to-target line, your left bicep touches the left side of your chest. The club head is above your wrists.

You're entering the impact zone.

We make no apologies for the detail, nor for repeating ourselves. That is exactly what you should be doing – studying the minutiae and dropping down into this position again and again.

Side-on, the left arm is connected to the chest, while the club shaft runs down the right forearm.

From the front the club head is above the hands, with the shaft still forming a 90-degree angle with the forearms, just prior to release.

117

A QUICK RECAP

HOW THE PROFESSIONALS DO IT

Now, though, let's draw in some finer detail to help you produce a professional-standard strike.

Again, the pictures on the opposite page (and shown from the side overleaf) are a repetition of those in Chapter 1. The checkpoints remain the same. The right hand unhinges and releases, taking the club shaft and head from above to below the hands, in an action similar to that of a hammer blow.

The wrists, acting as a lever, add real zip to the shaft and club head. The energy of the golf swing flows outwards, through the player's body and arms and into the club shaft (we focus on how to maximise this transfer of power later in the book).

At the same time, the core and hips rotate, with the arms still forming an inverted triangle up to the shoulders. The inside of the right elbow faces forward. The hands, arms and body are synchronised.

Releasing the hands correctly makes it possible to square the club. Fail to release the club, by retaining the lag, and you'll have to twist your body or wrists out of shape or pull your arms across your chest to try and contrive a square contact.

As the club approaches the ball, the face is half-square around two feet outside your right foot and nearly square by the time it passes your right toe (picture 1).

At impact, meanwhile, the hips have turned 45 degrees beyond square (picture 2), moving further round than they were at address (if they stopped turning, the arms and hands would become unstable – the hands would be held open in an effort to hit a straight shot, or flip over).

The left knee straightens, before moving out of the way to make room for the body to turn and the right hip to push laterally into the space vacated by the left. At no stage does the right hip drive out towards the ball and the ball-to-target line.

Post- and pre-impact positions are virtual carbon copies of each other (pictures 1 and 3). As you get beyond the ball, your hands continue on their arc – without rolling - and the arms maintain their inverted triangular shape and their radius.

Most poor golfers tend to dismiss what happens after impact as irrelevant – after all, the ball has already gone, hasn't it? So what if I hold my hands open or roll them over, come off the hand arc or change my radius after hitting the ball? It's too late to influence its direction or trajectory at this stage. If this is what you believe, think again.

Are you absolutely sure that these errors did not begin earlier? And even if you're right, these problems can quickly bleed back through your swing. Soon, let there be no doubt about it, problems occurring after impact will start affecting things that happen before.

(pictures 1–4) Pre- and post-impact positions are close copies of each other, with the club face remaining square to the ball well before and well after the strike due to the absence of hand roll.

1

2

3

4

→

1

The club face is almost square to the ball as it passes the right foot.

2

The hips have turned 45 degrees beyond square at impact.

3

The arms maintain their inverted triangle shape as well as their radius.

4

The hands continue swinging up the arc. They are about to start hinging up, but they are not rolling over.

COMPRESSION

At this point, though, we'd like to introduce an important new concept: compression. It sounds simple enough and it's often referred to. But many players spend their entire golfing lives never experiencing it.

Compression occurs at impact. It is the pressing of the club head down into the back of the ball, squeezing it against the ground and squeezing the ball away on a piercing trajectory. It's an action which not only produces a massively powerful strike but also a completely different sound to the 'slappy' impacts commonly heard among lesser players.

The right hand plays the major role. Once the club has released below the hands, the palm of the right hand starts squaring up to the ball. As it does so, and while continuing to follow the hand arc, it pushes downwards, thus adding mass to the speed of your swing. A club head may move fast into impact but it needs this extra pressure for a great strike.

Visually, what the right hand does is all but impossible to identify. It's a micro-move – but one that you'll definitely feel when you get it right. A downward press, it ensures that the hands stay ahead of the club head, causing a slight de-lofting of the face.

Try it. You'll be surprised how powerful your strike becomes once you supplement your hand release with a compressing of the ball. If you've never hit divots before, you will now. It's a move, and a sensation, that top players swear by.

To this add one further move. It involves the right forearm. Again, it is barely discernible and, for many golfers, involuntary. Technically, it is termed 'internal rotation'.

As emphasised in Chapter 1, the inside of the right elbow joint is facing forwards as it approaches the impact zone, with the elbow pointing at the right hip.

If the entire right arm now rotated anticlockwise, turning the right hand round in the process and leaving the elbow facing away from the target, that would be called 'external rotation'. That is not what we want.

'Internal rotation', in contrast, is a minute anticlockwise turn of the forearm only which, allied to the sensation of pressing down with the right hand, adds authority to the strike while also helping to finalise the squaring of the blade. It's a finishing touch, if you like. The sense is of the forearm making this small rotation independently, while the elbow retains its connection with the core. There should be no attempt to turn the right hand.

This movement has been highlighted in particular by the outstanding British golf coach Pete Cowen in recent years.

1 ✔

2 ✔

3 ✔

(pictures 1, 2 and 3)
These three pictures show compression and internal rotation. The hands are similar to their address position, with the back of the left hand slightly more bowed due to that compression.

BEST PRACTICE

1

Set up as normal...

2

...then press the right hand and right side of the body into the ball.

SIMULATING COMPRESSION

Here is a simple way to get the feel of compression. It resembles an isometric exercise.

Set up at address, with the head of your club aligned square against the bottom of, say, a door jamb or against an impact bag (picture 1). Now push the right side of your body to the left, simulating impact.

Push forwards with the palm of your right hand, so that the club head feels it is pressing both against the bag and down into the floor (picture 2). This action will also make the back of your left hand flatten or bow. The harder you press with your right hand, the more the shaft of your club will bend… and the more you'll feel what it is like to compress a golf ball.

WHERE 9 OUT OF 10 GOLFERS GO WRONG

HAND RELEASE: LEARNING TO LET GO

As we've already made clear, 9 out of 10 golfers roll their hands early on, sabotaging the rest of the swing in the process.

And most poor golfers overlay this error with yet more, whether it be by straying off the hand arc, disconnecting their arms from their core, by standing up or swaying laterally.

Here, though, we want to focus on those players with fundamentally sound swings – yet who still fail to release the club correctly. Arguably, 9 out of 10 players with reasonable swings still fail to do this!

"Most poor golfers tend to dismiss what happens after impact as irrelevant – after all, the ball has already gone, hasn't it? If this is what you believe, think again."

This golfer on the opposite page is a good example. He has not rolled his hands. His downswing has come from the inside and on a good plane, right down to the slot at the top of the impact zone.

All he has to do now is unhinge his wrists, allowing the club head to drop from above to below the hands and thus allowing it to start squaring up to the ball.

But he hasn't.

He's held on grimly to the lag as he enters the impact zone, trapping the club head above or just level with his hands. If he were releasing at this stage, the butt end of the club would point upwards. Instead it is parallel with the ground. He has retained the 90-degree angle between forearms and shaft. In not releasing, he is making it almost impossible to square up the club. Effectively, he's strangled his swing.

Try this position for yourself… and then try to square the club face at the moment of impact. You'll soon discover that the only way you can achieve this is by 'chicken-winging' and pulling your arms into your body – and all because of a failure to release and a loss of movement.

Now look at the golfer in the picture once more. You can see how static his hips have already become. They are square to the ball-to-target line when they should be opening out.

The majority of players who fail to release in this way display static hips. The core should be driving through and giving impetus to the swing. Instead, it's stopped. The arms, having lost their radius as well as their connection with the body, will now have to be dragged across the chest to deliver the best strike they can.

What about compression? Well, what about it? If you don't release the club, and if you don't square up the face, you can forget all about compression. You'll have to be satisfied with slapping the ball. Compression is simply not on the agenda.

What not to do: The core has stopped rotating, as have the hips, leading to a huge loss of power. This player will have to pull his arms across his chest to try and keep his swing moving.

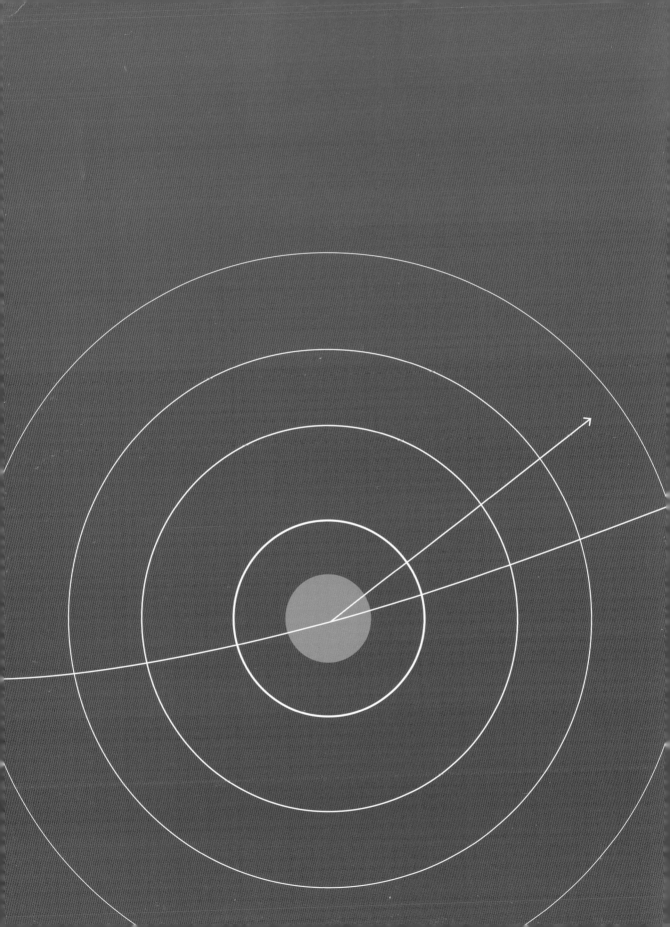

CHAPTER 10
A FINAL FOCUS ON HAND ARC AND HAND RELEASE

Hand release in the impact zone provides the key to unlocking good golf. Hand arc supplements it perfectly, dictating where the club head will be at every stage of the swing.

A FINAL FOCUS ON HAND ARC AND HAND RELEASE

…OR HOW TO PLAY GREAT GOLF STANDING ON ONE LEG!
Throughout this book we have unashamedly focused on the impact zone. Our message is clear – your golf game is going nowhere until you understand and master this key principle.

That also means mastering hand release, through wrist hinge rather than hand roll.

If we were asked, however, to highlight the next most important lesson for struggling players, we would not hesitate in emphatically replying: 'Hand arc, hand arc and more hand arc!'

Many players visiting Knightsbridge Golf School tell us they've never heard the term before. For us, it's a fundamental element of our teaching – it makes the golf swing much easier to both visualise and understand.

Hand arc is the route your hands should take during your golf swing. By definition, it also describes the direction that the arms take – the two, after all, are attached to each other. It also extends beyond the impact zone right through the swing.

It's not just about direction, though. It's about radius too. Keep your hands on their arc and the distance between them and the centre of your chest will remain constant as required.

There's an added bonus. Combine a good hand arc with the correct hand action and your club head will look after itself. Hand arc defines club head arc.

"Let's put it as bluntly as we can.

If you master the correct hand action

and blend that with a great hand arc,

you will have the whole package."

1

2

If your hand action is correct...

...and if you follow the hand arc, thus retaining the correct radius of your swing...

3

...then the club head will look after itself.

Many lesser players get fixated on the club head. They watch it suspiciously in the takeway and turn back and stare at it at the top of their practice swings. It's as if they are worried it might suddenly misbehave and disappear off on its own!

It never crosses their minds that the club head's position is largely determined by their hands. These golfers are looking in the wrong place. It's the hands they should be watching.

Let's put it as bluntly as we can.

If you master the correct hand action and blend that with a great hand arc, you will have the whole package. If your hand arc is good, and you know how to release your club correctly, you can play golf standing on one leg.

The best way to appreciate hand arc is to think of it in physical terms. Visualise it, then think of it as a material thing – for example a plastic or metal rail – suspended around your body.

Over the years, several training aids have tried to help guide and groove our golf swings. They've focused mainly on the club head arc. For us, the hand arc is far more important.

BEST PRACTICE

1

Set up with the end of the shaft against the wall.

2

The shaft will travel inside the wall on a gradual arc as the upper body turns.

3.

The hands have not rolled – they retain the same angles as they did at address as they follow the hand arc.

So let's try and create our own 'real' hand arc.

For this exercise, you won't need a full-length club – an empty grip would suit perfectly, although if you can get your local pro shop to cut down an old club to leave just a couple of inches protruding just below its grip, that would be even better. In place of either of those, you could also use a miniature children's club. But you will need a wall – a real one.

Take up your address position facing a wall (picture 1). You want to get close enough so that your hands – and your forehead – are almost touching it. If you had a club, it would need to pierce the wall in order to reach the ball.

Go through your takeaway in ultra slow motion. Your hands, without rolling or twisting, will gradually come off the wall on a mild arc as your arms move and your upper body turns (picture 2). Your arms, connected to the sides of your chest, retain the same radius. If they bent or cramped up, your hands would not be able to reach the hand arc.

Continue until your hands, as seen from along the ball-to-target line, are opposite your left hip and the shoulders have turned around 45 degrees (picture 3). Now turn over for steps 4–6.

→

The wrists begin to hinge.

The left arm swings up on a 45-degree line.

The hands, following the hand arc, touch or almost touch the wall at the top of the backswing.

Now turn around so that your backside touches the wall. Repeat the action, again in ultra slow motion, while still visualising – and feeling – the hand arc (picture 4).

From here, start hinging your wrists – remember, it's a mini, 'reactive' hinge which gradually increases throughout the backswing – as your arms swing up, the left one on a 45-degree line across your torso (picture 5).

As you approach the top in picture 6, your hands run into the wall. Since you're not holding a club, however, there is just enough room to complete your backswing behind your right shoulder.

Talented players seem to instinctively pick up the concept of hand arc. By some miracle, everything they do seems to work around the sense of a real, tangible hand arc suspended around their body.

That is why they, in contrast to lesser golfers, do not sway laterally or let their spine angle rise or fall. If their body swayed to the right in the backswing, for instance, while the hand arc remained in its original position, they'd sense immediately that their arms would not have enough space to swing up the arc correctly. So – naturally – they don't do it; they don't sway, stand up or dip.

Logically, it follows that if you know where your hands go during the swing, then that automatically sorts out the arms as well. It is impossible to over-extend or collapse the arms while keeping the hands on the arc at the same time.

1

Hitting the slot, as you enter the impact zone...

2

...the hands, keeping to their arc, have almost squared up to impact.

FOLLOWING THE HAND ARC BACK DOWN AGAIN

The downswing is, in effect, a repetition of the backswing. You simply return down the same hand arc. For the first few inches, the hands remain on the wall as the arms swing down and the shoulders all but remain fully turned. The arms then rejoin the 45-degree line.

Now turn around again and face the wall. Continue the downswing, still in ultra-slow motion, until the hands reach the 'slot' at the top of the impact zone.

You can use a full-length club this time, if you wish to practise the moment when the club head drops from above to below the hands to initiate the release. This is the start of the all important hand release. The club head will then mirror the squaring-up of the hands as it approaches the ball. If you use the cut-off club, however, you will be able to stand closer to the wall in front of you, thus practising the feeling of your hands brushing along it as they follow the perfect arc into impact. They return to where they started at address.

3

The palm of the right hand mirrors the square club face at impact, ensuring a straight shot.

4

The club face stays flush square to the wall just beyond impact, since the hands have not rolled.

Now practise this move into the ball, and the impact position, by turning side-on to the wall and pushing your left side up against it. Why are we carrying out these drills next to a wall? Simple. You can't argue with walls!

If, during the takeaway, your hands immediately collide with the wall then, clearly, you've already gone wrong. And you can't argue if your hands immediately roll inside, way off the wall. You've obviously come off the arc.

Spin your shoulders open at the start of the downswing while facing the wall and your

hands will strike the wall. You'll also quickly realise you've slipped off the hand arc if, standing with your left shoulder up against the wall, your chicken-winging left elbow makes contact with bricks and mortar while your hands, having trapped their release, are still hinged or have rolled backwards.

We always use video at Knightsbridge to help our students study their swings. We draw lines onto the pictures for guidance. The wall drill, however, seems to be a quicker, more effective way of helping players who struggle with the idea of hand arc. It's like colliding with reality.

The hands come off the wall gradually, mirroring the takeaway.

The hands continue along their arc, with the arms naturally extended.

The hands start to hinge rather than roll – another mirror position.

TEE TIME

To complete the exercise, take a grip or handle with a short section of shaft sticking out. Add a tee, either pushing it into the hole at the top of the grip if you're using on of the options on page 135, or fixing it with Blu-Tack if you have improvised with an alternative household item.

Turn back and face the wall front on. Simulate impact, with your hands and forehead all but touching the wall. Then slowly continue swinging your hands along the hand arc beyond impact.

HITTING THE WALL

Your hands will gradually come inside and off the wall (picture 1), the inverted triangle of your naturally extended arms still in shape, before the left arm softens and folds up so as not to block the movement (picture 3). The hands will gradually hinge up, perfectly mirroring what happened earlier in the backswing, as the right arm swings up on a 45-degree line across the chest.

Again, if your hands or elbows run into the wall straight after impact, you must have failed to release your hands and square them up correctly. You may have stayed on the hand arc in the downswing, but you've certainly come off it now.

Alternatively, you may chicken-wing into impact and then draw your hands sharply into your body and away from the wall (with this fault, it would be more effective – and striking! – to practise the throughswing with your back to the wall).

Notice that in both situations the arms have buckled and cramped upwards. They've lost radius.

Virtually all bad shots involve a loss or change of radius. In other words, virtually all bad shots involve the hands straying off the hand arc at some point.

ARE YOU REALLY READY TO HANDLE HAND RELEASE?

1 ✔

The tee points to the core...

2 ✔

...then to the right hip...

And now for our final thoughts on hand release. Again, we make no apologies for repetition. You can't repeat correct hand release enough.

Let's now approach things this time from another, less conventional angle to ensure the penny has dropped.

We launched this book by beginning with the impact zone, after all, rather than with the more usual introduction of grip, posture and set-up. We felt that that back-to-front approach made real sense. And we've also replaced your clubs at times with frying pans or tennis rackets, and invited you to hit walls, both real and imaginary. So why not continue in the same unconventional vein?

Let's opt again for the grip or handle, with a short section of shaft sticking out. This time, though, use the tee peg stuck into the top of the handle as a pointer... and simply

3 ✔

...then parallel along the wall.

4 ✘

If your hands roll, the tee will immediately betray you!

repeat the 'wall drill' from earlier in this chapter (pages 134-35).

Set up again, facing the wall as before, with the bottom end of the handle touching or almost touching the wall. Carry out the takeaway. And watch the tee peg.

It should begin pointing towards your core (picture 1). Then, as your arms move and your body turns, it should gradually point towards your right hip area (picture 2). As

your hands get to waist height, opposite your left hip, the tee should now point parallel to the wall (picture 3). If you've achieved this, you've not rolled or twisted your hands. You're in great shape. But if your tee peg is now pointing directly at the wall (picture 4), then you have. And you aren't.

This handle drill is excellent for helping players to grasp how the hands directly affect the club head… even when there is no club head to be seen. It's also a perfect way of highlighting hand roll.

As explained earlier, many golfers fixate on the club head and forget all about their hands. Far better to fixate on the handle instead.

Now turn around, touching the wall with your backside. Continue your backswing. Start with a mini-hinge of the wrists, then swing your arms up on the 45-degree line. With your hands following the hand arc, the tee will point downwards on a similar angle, somewhere between your feet and the ball-to-target line (picture 1).

Roll your hands clockwise, though, and the tee will point way beyond the ball-to-target line

Completing your backswing, the hands run into the wall behind your right shoulder. Continued far enough and the now fully-hinged handle will end up parallel with the wall (picture 2).

Now go into reverse. With your shoulders still fully turned, your arms swing down the wall for a couple of inches – in slow motion – before returning on the same 45-degree angle, as explained in the previous drill.

Halfway down, the tee points close to the ball-to-target line. It still does at waist level where the hands still hold a 90-degree hinge between your forearms and your (imaginary!) club shaft.

Your hands then intersect with the point, or 'slot', where you began hinging your wrists during the backswing.

"If you know where your hands go during the swing, then that automatically sorts out the arms as well. It is impossible to over-extend or collapse the arms while keeping the hands on the arc at the same time."

Halfway up and the tee points between the feet and ball-to-target line.

At the top, the tee points parallel to the wall.

1

2

The tee points down at the ball-to-target line as it enters the impact zone...

...then points up at your left hip as your hands release.

TAKE THE LIE DETECTOR TEST!

This handle-and-peg drill really comes into its own as it enters and exits the impact zone. Again, there's no better way to illustrate whether or not a player has mastered hand release. It's like a lie detector test. You can't beat it.

As you enter the impact zone, the hands start releasing. The bottom end of the handle moves from pointing above the hands (picture 1) to below (picture 2). Then the hands, synchronised with the body, turn and begin to square up to the ball.

The tee in the handle perfectly reflects this crucial stage by changing direction dramatically. From pointing down at the line of the ball as the hands enter the impact zone, the tee now points at the left hip.

That rapid change confirms that a correct release and squaring-up has been initiated.

As the release continues into impact, frame by frame, the tee points ever closer to the centre of your core, from where it started (picture 3).

Just beyond impact, with the inverted triangle of the arms retaining its shape, the tee gradually starts to point into your right side (picture 4), a mirror image of the pre-impact position.

3

The tee now points at your core...

4

...then towards your right side.

This is a crucial checkpoint for players who never fully release their hands or allow the club shaft to get past their hands. Indeed, it may come as a big shock to people who think they do.

Complete this part of the drill by turning sideways, with your left shoulder pressed to the wall. Go back to the impact zone, then release and square up the hands. The left arm, left hand and handle all meet the wall flush at the moment of impact.

(In reality, if you are using an iron rather than a wood, your hands would be a fraction ahead of the ball at impact, thus leaving the club shaft leaning slightly forward. But this part of the drill is all about experiencing the sensation of a squared-up hand and club position.)

The back of your left hand aligns perfectly with the flat surface of the wall at impact, as would – if you were using a normal-length club – the leading edge of the club head.

All these positions mirror what happened pre-impact, the tee pointing into your right side...

...then parallel to the wall...

...then down to the ball-to-target line.

Now face the wall again and put the finishing touches to the exercise by swinging past impact. Again, these positions mirror what has happened before, with the hands and handle staying on the arc.

The bottom end of the handle gradually comes off the wall, swinging inside it as the hands follow the hand arc. Note how the triangle of the arms remains in shape. Note also, in pictures 1, 2 and 3, how the hands have been fully released. If this golfer had a full-length club, the club head would have overtaken the hands after impact.

Continuing to waist height, the bottom end of the handle is pointing parallel to the wall, before the hands begin to hinge upwards (picture 3) and the left arm softens and folds so as not to impede the movement.

THE DOOR FRAME

At first sight, the picture sequence on the left and continued overleaf duplicates those set against the wall in the preceding section of this chapter.

By enclosing our golfer within the limited space of a door frame, however, where he is forced to use a club handle rather than a full-length club, we have redoubled the focus on his hand action. We've also made it more difficult for him to stray off the hand arc without ending up with bruised hands!

Why concentrate so much on the hands? Because it reminds you that they dictate what happens to the club head. Perfect hand action equals a perfect club head.

The door frame has the added advantage of providing a set of physical references all around the golfer's body. The end of the handle, for instance, all but touches the frame in front of the golfer as his backside touches it behind (picture 1). In the takeaway, the handle swings inside the door frame (picture 2). If it swings outside, then the action's wrong – and you'll damage your knuckles in the process.

These reference points are available throughout the swing. You can see where your hands should be, in relation to the sides and top of the frame, at any point. As you start to hinge after the takeaway, your hands will be between a third and half of the way across the door (picture 3), around halfway, or just over halfway across it as they follow the hand arc up to your chest (picture 4) and almost fully across and next to the door jamb behind you as you reach the top (picture 5).

→

Similar reference points will be available during the downswing – halfway back down and the hands are halfway across the frame, for instance (picture 7). See also how picture 11 is a close copy of picture 1, only with the added dynamism of the core and hips opening up towards the target.

So this is not just a wooden door frame, it's a golfing frame of reference! It's like the lines that golf instructors like to draw on videos of their golfers to try and encapsulate their swings.

Only this way, the feedback is much more physical and much less theoretical.

Go slow, though. Look after those hands.

WHERE 9 OUT OF 10 GOLFERS GO WRONG

1

2

What not to do: This golfer looks in a reasonable position entering the impact zone, but his core and hips are grinding to a halt rather than turning through.

What not to do: His core and hips are still square just before impact, while his hands are not releasing – the tee tells the story, still pointing forwards past his left hip.

THE TEE TELLS THE STORY!

Above is a player who, through failing to release, has completely wrecked his swing in the latter stages. We see this sort of swing all the time. Following the handle-and-peg sequence shown above makes it crystal clear where he's going wrong.

We've extended this sequence to include the entire impact zone rather than just a few frames before and after impact.

Coming into the zone, he's in good shape at waist height, although the hips are already looking static. But the failure to release and square up the hands means his tee does not change direction dramatically as it should.

Instead of turning to point into the left hip and then the core, the tee – reflecting the fact that the club and shaft are trapped behind the hands – points beyond the ball and almost down the fairway.

3

4

What not to do: The arms are beginning to buckle, losing their radius and causing the hands to lift up, inside the hand arc.

What not to do: The dreaded chicken wing appears! The arms are not extending, while the tee now points behind the left side of the torso.

The inverted triangle of the arms loses shape and they buckle up, losing their radius. The hips grind to a halt and fail to get past square to the ball-to-target line. The arms, still moving fast, drag across the chest.

The tee, meanwhile, never turns in to point at the core or at the right thigh upon completion of release. It can't. Instead it points past the left thigh, then round

and behind the left side of the chest as the chicken wing gets more and more pronounced.

By the end of this sequence, this player has committed two cardinal sins. He has failed to release his hands, and he has come off the hand arc. And the handle makes that perfectly clear.

You may wonder why players who appear to hinge their hands correctly in the backswing, then stay on the hand arc during the downswing – as opposed to those who get out of position through rolling their hands early – still fail to release their hands.

We do too!

Perhaps it's instinctive. Perhaps they feel their arms and club shaft swinging down on a 45-degree angle towards the ball and see no way of changing the angle of their approach.

Instead of releasing the hands and squaring them up to the ball, they continue downwards on the same 45-degree path, the heel of the club leading into impact and thus hitting the ball straight right with an open club face.

Perhaps they get confused by the angles. At waist height, after all, the club faces a full 90 degrees away from where it wants to be facing at impact. So, not understanding how release and squaring-up works, they improvise and compensate.

Or perhaps, because the ball is round and without a flat edge, they simply fail to grasp that for it to fly straight, the ball must be struck with a flat club face that is square to the ball-to-target line.

Striking an impact bag with a club – or a carpet with a carpet beater – might help alter this perception. In those cases, it's easier to feel that one flat surface must be met flush by another flat surface. After all, it would make no sense hitting a carpet with the edge of a carpet beater rather than its face.

Alternatively, simply use a club handle. Pay attention to how the butt end behaves. It works wonders to help you remember the key principle:

Hand arc defines club head arc. If your hand arc is good, and you know how to release and square up your club correctly, you can play golf standing on one leg.

CHAPTER 11
THE FINISH

A correct finish not only looks majestic –
it confirms all the good things that have
occurred earlier in the swing. A bad finish,
though, betrays fatal errors which can
often be traced back to long before impact.

THE FINISH

ARE YOU A COUNTERFEIT?
Question: Which of the three swings on the right represent a good finish?

Answer: Certainly picture 1 and picture 2, even if they are not 'full'.

But certainly not picture 3.

Picture 3 is a full finish that is not quite what it seems. It's masquerading as a full finish. It's a fake, mirroring the fake backswing we discussed earlier (see page 82).

Many full finishes are counterfeit, even ones that look better than the one depicted in picture 3. Some look perfectly posed. But they can be just that – posed and little more than artificial add-ons.

The key questions to ask are: Did the hands follow the hand arc after impact? Did the arms extend through as the ball was struck? Did the core drive the body as it turned through to the finish?

In picture 3, the answer is an emphatic 'no'.

Picture 1, incidentally, depicts a half finish and picture 2 a three-quarter finish. And yes, here the hands have remained on their arc, the arms have kept the same radius – they have not shortened or bent at the elbow – and the body has kept turning. In both cases, the golfer has delivered an accurate, powerful strike.

1

A half finish – the body turns through, the hands follow the hand arc and the arms retain their radius.

A technically correct three-quarter finish will invariably send the ball further than a full but flawed finish. It's a lesson that many golfers find hard to digest.

Just think back to Darren Clarke's hugely impressive 2011 victory at The Open at Royal St George's. He won that week

2

A three-quarter finish – the same again, only with more body turn and a longer hand arc.

3

A fake finish – the body fails to turn fully, the hands come inside the perfect hand arc and the arms thus lose their radius.

through pinpoint accuracy – and by abbreviating his finishes. It's not a new idea, of course. The controlled, precise three-quarter finish, so useful on tricky golf courses or in particularly windy conditions, has been taught at Knightsbridge for more than 50 years.

Every fake finish tells you one thing. Something has gone wrong earlier in the swing. As we said before, errors tend to bleed backwards. A bad finish may have started going wrong way, way back – even before impact, indeed.

1

The triangle retains its shape, the arms retain their connection.

2

The hands stay on the hand arc – without rolling.

PICTURE-PERFECT FINISHES
So here's the correct way to do it.

You've just come out of the impact zone as shown in picture 1, with your club horizontal to the ground. This is the half finish. The inverted triangle formed by your arms and shoulders remains intact and in shape. The arms are still connected to the sides of your chest. Some players may be starting to slightly hinge their hands up at this stage, but it should not feel like a 'forced' or intentional action.

Your head has not moved and is still at the same height. You have not started looking up or standing up. Your hips are facing the target, or almost so. Your right knee has

3

A powerful core rotation and centrifugal force help complete the full finish.

By the time you have reached the three-quarter finish, the body and hips are facing the target, the right foot is balanced on its toes, the knees are tight together, with the right one pointing down the fairway. Your weight has transferred onto your left leg.

Note the hands and the arms. If, as in picture 2, your hands have not twisted, they will still be on their arc and you will have maintained your arm radius, with the left arm folding and the right arm extended.

moved laterally to all but touch your left knee. Your left leg is firm and straight.

Stop at this point and you'd be amazed how far the ball would go. But there's another good reason to stop here during your practice sessions – it gives you the perfect opportunity to check on the elements of the swing that we have listed above.

The final picture completes the turn, with the arms relaxing as they decelerate. A powerful core movement and centrifugal force running down the arms and through to the club head has pulled the golfer's body to this point.

WHERE 9 OUT OF 10 GOLFERS GO WRONG

YOU'RE ONLY FOOLING YOURSELF
Compare the previous finish (see pages 162-63) to the 'fake' finish shown in the following pictures. Here, as seen in both pictures 1 and 2, there has been no driving core movement and very little centrifugal force. The body has stalled and the arms are doing their best to maintain some impetus to the swing. All of these issues can be traced back to a much earlier point in the swing – in some cases to the very beginning!

This golfer, in all probability, was already out of shape and in a poor position as he came into the impact zone, thus blocking a correct hand and body release. Alternatively, he may have produced a good backswing and downswing, only to fail to release his hands at the crucial moment, his swing thus grinding to a halt.

Whatever preceded this position, however, it is now up to his arms and hands to pull something out of the fire.

Coming out of the impact zone, the arms are no longer forming an inverted triangle – they have been pulled out of shape. They are no longer connected to the chest and they lose their radius as they collapse. The hands – and the club head – are not on their arc.

The one thing you can say in favour of this 'method'? That at least it allowed our golfer to make some sort of contact with the ball. At least, we hope so.

1

What not to do: The left arm is 'chicken-winging'...

2

...there's a loss of radius as the hands roll over...

3

...and the elbows splay as the arms collapse.

BEST PRACTICE

Address the ball, lift your arms, turn through to the target – this is the best way to learn the feeling of your hands not rolling.

THE SIMPLEST OF CHECK-UPS

It's easy to check whether you're rolling your hands or collapsing your arms during the throughswing.

Set yourself up at address, then simply lift up your arms to waist height while keeping your body down. Now turn your body to the left to face the target. Your hands will not have twisted, nor will your arms have changed their radius.

Bank this feeling. Then try to hang onto it during your full swing.

Incidentally, by turning right instead of left you can reproduce the feeling you want to experience during the backswing. Again, no hand roll, with the arms still set in their triangle.

Simple, isn't it?

AND FINALLY...

GIVE THE LEADING EDGE ONE LAST LOOK

Once you have swung to the finish – whether it be to a three-quarter or to a full finish – well, you've finished, right?

Not quite. We'd like to give you one further move to build into your swing. It's not so much an exercise as a swing check that we'd like you to adopt as second nature.

Having completed your follow-through, drop your hands back down towards hip level. The club shaft should now be parallel with the ball's line of flight, the club head above the hands on an angle of 45 degrees and pointing after the ball. Its face should be around eye level – in the perfect position, indeed, to check on where it is pointing.

If the leading edge is vertical, then you've probably hit a straight shot. If it's not, then you very probably didn't, instead either rolling your hands – and club face – to the left or twisting them to the right.

The lesson is simple.

The easiest way to split fairways and knock down flags is to keep the club face square to your body throughout the golf swing.

Checking that the leading edge of the club face is vertical; make this part of your routine after each shot.

CHAPTER 12
POWER GOLF

Power flows outwards through the golf
swing, from the core through the arms,
through hand release, the shaft, and into
the club head. Used correctly and in the
right sequence, these elements combine
to produce a magical effect on the strike
of the ball.

POWER GOLF

Have you ever wondered how a whip produces its crack? It's hard to believe, but that sound is actually a mini sonic boom. You make a controlled body, arm and wrist movement at one end of the whip, and moments later its tip is breaking the sound barrier…

Golfers should take note. There's something similar going on in the golf swing. Or, at least, there should be.

So what's the key to golfing power?

"A powerful golf shot, like the crack of a whip, is all about generating speed and then successfully transferring it into the club head."

Power is a direct result of good fundamentals, a structured swing and the outward transfer of energy.

Throughout this book we've focused on building a correct swing pattern. That has meant concentrating on individual body, arm, hand and club positions, and repeating them correctly and consistently before blending them into short, defined, slow-motion actions. We see these positions as crucial signposts along your route to becoming a fine golfer.

Ultimately, however, the swing is dynamic rather than static. It's all about motion – and high-speed motion at that.

So now is the time to inject power into the structure.

A powerful golf shot, like the crack of a whip, is all about generating speed and then successfully transferring it into the club head. Many golfers manage the first part of this equation without paying heed to the second.

As with the whipping action, speed originates from the centre and surges outwards, gaining momentum and multiplying through a series of levers and a well-timed sequence before striking the ball.

THE CORE

The core is not just the area of the abdomen seen from the front.

Imagine it as a belt of muscle wrapping right around the front, sides and back of the torso.

A BELT OF MUSCLE

The core represents the heart of your golf swing. Most people think of the abdomen as their core. We, though, see it as the entire belt of muscle extending from the stomach area at the front of the body right round to the spine at the back.

This is the area that fires your downswing into life after the transition. The core, by beginning to turn over a solid and grounded lower body, sets off the chain reaction. There is no tugging of the shoulders or throwing open of the hips. The core leads the way.

THE PRESSURE

The human piledriver – Tiger Woods reaches the top of his backswing...

...then drives his entire body weight down into the ground in search of traction and power.

SO GROUNDED!

As the core turns and the arms drop, the lower body continues the feeling, begun in the transition, of pressing hard down into the ground.

This pressure, or sense of feeling 'grounded', is crucial to power. If you lift up your body in the downswing, you are jettisoning this all-important traction with the ground, as well as your chance of truly compressing the ball.

Picture a boxer or a javelin thrower. They plant their lower body before exploding into action. Now imagine them, but this time hanging in mid-air from a harness. Without the leverage they normally get through their feet, they're robbed of their power. No pressure, no knock-out punch.

THE CONNECTION

THE TRANSMISSION SYSTEM
With pressure must come speed.

If the core is the generator, then the arms, set in their 'inverted triangle', represent the transmission system. The two must be connected.

Imagine turning your core rapidly but losing the connection with the arms. The core and hips, then chest and shoulders would rip round towards the ball, leaving the arms struggling behind and having to find their own way into impact. Alternatively the arms, tugging themselves out of their triangular shape, could set off on their own, with the core stalling completely and failing to turn.

Either way, there wouldn't be any outward flow of power from the centre down the arms. The core and the arms would be acting independently of each other.

Put another way, the rotating heart of the wheel would no longer be attached to the rim.

The feeling of the biceps being connected to the sides of the chest must be maintained throughout the downswing and beyond if you are going to successfully transfer the power of your body movement into the club via your arms. (It is equally important, of course, to keep your arms feeling active and alive. Active, fluid muscles move faster than taut, rigid ones.)

The turn of the body adds speed to the arm swing – but only if the biceps are connected to the walls of the upper chest.

Picture two cogs. If their teeth are engaged, power flows from one to the other. Disengaged, they'll spin around independently. It would be a bit like pushing on the accelerator of a car while keeping the clutch down.

A lot of noise and no drive. Much ado about nothing.

THE LEVER

1

2

4

5

3

(pictures 1–5)
Using the wrists and hands as a lever confirms what you have learnt previously about release and the unhinging of the wrists.

THE WHIP EFFECT
The final element of power is provided by the wrists. They don't just transfer the speed which has come surging out of the core and down the arms into the club head and the ball. They multiply it.

This sequence highlights perfectly what is happening. Look at the hands in picture 1. Now look at the hands in picture 5. How far have they travelled along their arc? Perhaps a foot? Now look at the club head in both picture 1 and 5. It has travelled five or six times that distance, in exactly the same time. It follows that it is moving five or six times as fast – and all because of release and the use of the wrist lever.

The science of levers is simple to demonstrate. Take a club shaft or a cane (you don't want a heavy club to illustrate this) and swing it horizontally at chest level while keeping your wrists rigid. Now remove all tension from your wrist muscles and swing again. Which swing produced the louder swish?

Similarly, no one would try to crack a whip with a stiff wrist. We have, of course, covered this movement when discussing hand release. Synchronised with your body turn, the releasing wrist is the final lever available to you in your quest for power.

It gives your swing, well, real whip.

THE SEQUENCE

GETTING THINGS IN THE RIGHT ORDER

Poor golfers often refer to a loss of timing to explain away their bad shots. Often this is a cop-out. Timing sounds like some sort of magical, whimsical ingredient, something out of the player's control and which comes and goes as it chooses.

'Sequence' would be a much better word to use. And getting the sequence right is very much in your control.

To retain the power you create in your downswing, you must not only use the correct parts of your body while passing through the correct positions, but you must also do everything in the correct order. The feet press down, the core leads, the connected arms follow and the wrist delivers the pay-off.

Getting the sequence right takes us right back to the transition in Chapter 7 – the slowest part of the swing which so many lesser golfers rush through without even noticing.

If you fail to allow your arms to drop smoothly at this point, and also fail to press down through the left foot while bumping back across to the target, you'll lose the sequence before your downswing has really got going.

We mentioned our javelin thrower earlier in this chapter. Can you imagine him trying to throw while still running, and only planting his front foot after he had let go of the javelin. Getting things in the wrong order like this would also mean he wouldn't be able to turn his body through.

So not only would his throw look all wrong, but the javelin wouldn't go very far either.

It's the same with the golf swing. Get out of sequence and you'll get yourself into unfamiliar territory. More than this, one error will also lead to another, compounding the problem.

If you start your downswing by spinning your shoulders round and over the top, for instance, you'll also force your arms to become disconnected.

The bottom line is that your strike will be compromised. Like the athlete who tries to throw his javelin while still on the run, you'll lose out on distance while also losing out on accuracy.

Get all these elements right and something magical happens, as shown in the two pictures opposite.

THE MAGIC!

1

First, the club catches up with the hands through impact, the right arm and club shaft forming a straight line...

2

...then the club overtakes the hands (the right arm and the shaft are no longer aligned) through sheer centrifugal force. It's a magical feeling!

CENTRIFUGAL FORCE TAKES OVER

At some point after releasing your hands, you suddenly sense that it is the club head which is leading you whereas, earlier in the swing, it was you leading it. The club shaft has released from its lagged position, the action feels as if it has been widened and expanded, and centrifugal force takes over.

One moment you're swinging the club, then it overtakes you, as if it had a life – or motion – of its own. Take a look at really long drivers of the golf ball. Having fired through with their core, all the power seems to flood outwards, through the arms and into the club head at the rim of the swing.

WHERE 9 OUT OF 10 GOLFERS GO WRONG

IT'S ALL ABOUT ENERGY TRANSFER!

None of the magic on pages 176-77 happens to poor golfers. There is no transfer of energy from the inside to the outside. They may appear to move their bodies quickly, but none of that speed is transferred to the club head and, ultimately, to the ball.

What are they doing wrong? It could be almost anything. They may be missing one of the key elements, whether it's the use of their core, the push into the ground, the connection or the release of their wrists. Often they do things out of sequence, or their swings may simply contain basic errors – like hand roll rather than wrist hinge – leading them into trapped, static positions from which they cannot escape.

Any of these factors will block the outward flow of energy.

Indeed, the energy and speed intended for the club head can be forced into reverse, travelling back up the arms and into the body. It's a bit like the effect on a driver as his car smashes into a barrier.

DON'T REVERSE THE FLOW!

Look, for instance, at the golfer above. Having failed to turn his core and release his hands, his arms have lost their triangular shape and begun to chicken-wing, with the left elbow bowing out towards the target.

The whole action is now blocked. The speed that should have flowed into the ball must

What not to do: Where has all the energy gone? Certainly not into the club head – this swing, in fact, has gone into reverse.

go somewhere, so it travels back up the braced arms and into the torso. The brakes are on. In some cases, you even see the golfer's head jerk upwards as a reaction. It's almost painful to watch.

Expect a weak, topped shot as a result – and a sore neck. Don't expect any crack of the whip.

BEST PRACTICE – PART I

CAN YOU HEAR THE 'SWISH'?

Get hold of a club shaft or cane. Set up normally, then carry out a few slow mini-swings extending from, say, the start to the end of the impact zone. Keep your arms and your grip active and alive, rather than tense or taut, and make sure you turn your core back and through.

Slowly increase the speed of these mini-swings. Don't stop between them. Just swing through and then back, like a pendulum. Retain your connection as well as your weight into the ground. Let your hands release as you would in a full swing.

Now – can you hear the swish of the shaft as it swings through and back?

Enjoy it – for that is the sound of energy flowing out from your core, down your arms, through your hand release and into the shaft.

If this exercise sounds familiar, go back to the introduction of this book. It's an exact duplication of what we said the pros do at the start of their warm-ups. They, as we highlighted, are reacquainting themselves with the impact zone.

But the exercise is just as good for acquainting yourself with the feeling of your golf swing's energy, as it flows from core to club head, from centre to rim.

"To retain the power you create in your downswing, you must not only use the correct parts of your body while passing through the correct positions, but you must also do everything in the correct order. The feet press down, the core leads, the connected arms follow and the wrist delivers the pay-off."

BEST PRACTICE – PART II

LET YOUR SWING 'EXPAND' AND GO!

As in the previous exercise, find a golf shaft without a club head. You don't want any weight at the end of the shaft for this drill. Set yourself at address but without bending forwards from the hips. Hold the shaft in your left hand.

Draw your left arm across your chest towards your right shoulder and hinge your wrist, but without turning your torso. Imagine you are handling a sword. Now lash the shaft through impact at waist level, again not using any body movement. Keep your arm free of tension. Feel the angle of your wrist-hinge expand outwards as the shaft gains momentum through impact. If you feel this 'expansion' correctly, you will not have pulled, or chicken-winged, with the left arm.

Now repeat the motion while adding body turn. Your left arm will now stretch further back. Swing back through.

You'll produce a surprising amount of extra force thanks to the body rotation and extra leverage. You'll sense this power flowing out from your lower back as it unwinds. It will pass through the muscles around your left shoulder, through your arm, wrist and into the shaft.

It's a remarkably free movement. Previously, you've focused on setting your body and club into static positions. Here, you're relying on rotation, arm movement and wrist release to create an accurate, fast and powerful club arc.

Now try the same thing, swinging through from right to left while using only your right arm. Then do so with both arms, set in their inverted triangle. Keep them feeling active, fluid and alive.

Whereas you may previously have tugged or pushed, thus blocking a free-flowing movement, you're now experiencing the same forces created and felt by all good players. Only by winding up the body to its fullest, then releasing these accumulated forces in an expanding motion – like an uncoiling spring – can you swing the golf club easily, naturally and with maximum power.

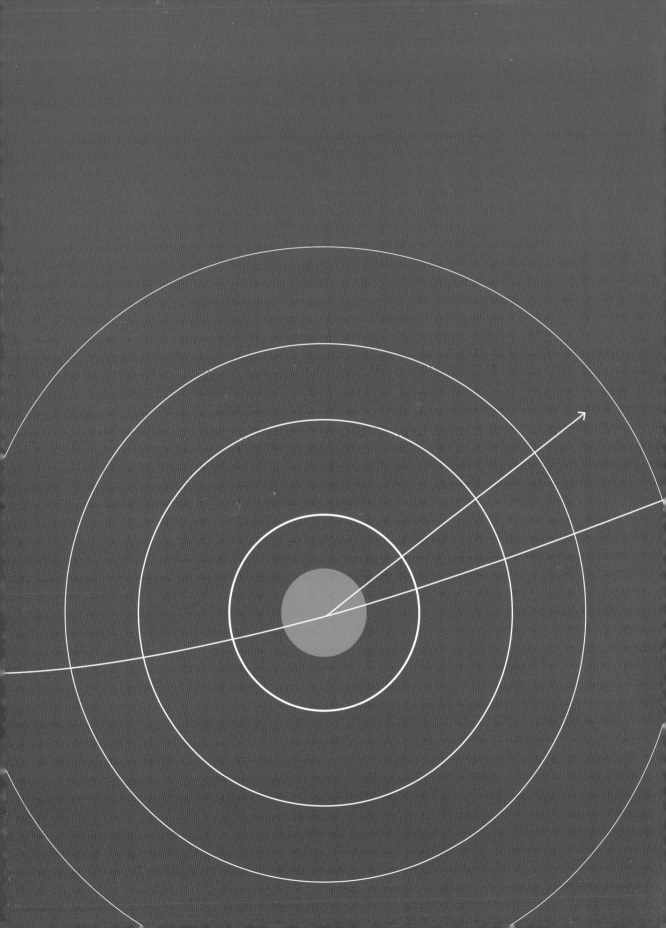

CHAPTER 13
THE (NOT SO) SHORT GAME

The short game is often taught as a completely different technique. Wouldn't it be much easier, though, if it were directly related to the long game? What if a chip and a pitch were little more than the impact zone itself?

THE (NOT SO) SHORT GAME

This book is not about the short game. It's about the full swing.

So why are we including a section on chipping and pitching?

Because – if you follow our system and our philosophy – you can't have one without the other. You can't have a long game without the short.

Many lesser players struggle with their short games because of what they mistakenly believe is the only method. They think they have to open their stance, play the ball off their back foot, open the face and swing from out to in. That way, so the theory goes, you'll cut across the ball and add spin and check.

"The chip is just a mini version of the impact zone. And so is the pitch – only with a bit more wrist hinge. It's that simple."

Perhaps. If you get it just right. More likely, though, you'll duff or shank the shot.

We don't see chipping like that.

For us, the chip is just a mini version of the full swing, or, more exactly, a mini version of the impact zone. And so is the pitch – only with a bit more wrist hinge. It's that simple.

'Simple', indeed, is the word we want to stress throughout this chapter.

Why confuse yourself? Why struggle to adopt a completely new technique when a mini impact zone – something you've already learnt to do and learnt to trust in your long game – will do the job perfectly in 95 per cent of cases?

Sure, if you're chipping onto the billiard-table greens of Augusta or playing out of Muirfield's pothole bunkers on a daily basis, you'll need to learn a few 'speciality' shots. But our method is perfect for most situations. That's why most good players – and many professionals, too – rely on it 95 per cent of the time.

For the most part, if you want a great short game all you need to do is focus on impact. There's a chip or pitch hiding in every golf swing. The same rules and the same fundamentals apply. Every shot, after all, is about perfect striking. Golf's that simple.

THE CHIP

1

The stance is square, the ball is centred between the heels.

2

The hands do not roll – note how the concave shape at the back of the right hand has been retained.

3

The arms keep their inverted triangle shape.

A MINI IMPACT ZONE

A chip, therefore, is a mini impact zone – so mini that it does not include wrist hinge. It barely deviates from our swing model.

Start with a normal, square address position, but open the club a fraction before taking your grip – and we mean a fraction! This will allow the club head to skid off the ground rather than snag if the contact is not quite perfect. We all need a little forgiveness now and then.

The length of the club will mean your shaft is slightly more upright and you are more over the ball.

Position the ball in the middle of your heels as shown in picture 1. Then, and only then, point your left toe slightly – and again, we mean just slightly! – to the left. This will make the ball seem further back in your stance. Trust us – it isn't.

Your hands will be just to the left, or ahead of, the ball (see picture 2), thus promoting a descending blow and making it easier to get the club head under the ball. Feel a little more weight in your left side – just a little, say 60 per cent of your total body weight.

Start your takeaway as you would with a full shot. Your arms swing back, the wrists retain their angles without rolling, the right shoulder rotates back and around the spine. The action of the right shoulder brings the arms inside on a mild arc. It allows the club face to remain square in relation to the body turns, and automatically lifts the club

→

1

Viewing the sequence on the previous pages from side-on, there is no appreciable wrist hinge.

2

The right hand presses down into the ball – listen for a perfect impact!

3

The core turns through, in unison with the arm swing.

as well. There is no appreciable wrist hinge. On the way down, the core turns back, with the arms connected. There is a feeling of pressing down with the right hand – you will sense this in your right index finger. The hands are slightly – slightly! – ahead of the club head. This feeling of pressing down continues through impact as the ball is compressed.

Listen. You can hear a good impact as much as you can feel one.

The hands, arms and core are all synchronised. The core keeps turning through (see picture 3), transferring the weight into the left side and causing a slight hip turn by the finish. The arms retain their inverted triangle shape and the club head finishes low to the ground, below the hands. The hands have followed the same arc as in the full swing. There has been no hand roll.

Good players often say they feel as if they chip with their chests. They push the club down with their hands, squeezing the ball away, while turning through with the chest. The arms, through connection, go along with that movement.

For short chips, or chipping on very fast greens, lighten your grip pressure from 6 or 7 out of 10 to 4 or 5 or even lower. That will soften the strike and reduce the distance.

If you need the ball to roll more, use a more straight-faced club rather than changing your action. Is there anything odd about chipping with, say, a 5-iron from the edge of a large green?

No. Top players do it. So should you.

THE PITCH

THE CHIP'S BIG BROTHER

If the chip is a mini impact zone, then the pitch is its big brother.

For us, the only real difference between chipping and pitching is the addition of wrist break, arm lift and a bit more turn – just like the takeaway in the full swing.

Pitches tend to be hit harder and fly further and higher than chips. They tend to stop quicker, because of the additional backspin. But, fundamentally, pitches are an extended impact zone – they're a big chip (with added wrist hinge) or, seen from the opposite angle, a mini full swing. Proving the point that chips, pitches and the full swing are the closest of relations.

Addressing a pitch is similar to addressing a chip. The feet are still close but have edged slightly further apart. The ball is still in the middle of the heels. Again, the left foot is splayed slightly open, to help the body clear after impact, the butt of the club is in line with the ball or just a fraction ahead and, again, you may feel a little more weight on your left side, as in picture 1.

The takeaway is the same, only longer. And as it extends, a small, micro wrist hinge (see picture 2) is introduced. This action occurs as the hands pass the right thigh. There is no hand roll – the leading edge and face of the club remain square to the body. The body turns throughout (see picture 3)

1

(pictures 1, 2 and 3)
The ball is still in the middle of the heels but may appear to be further back due to the left foot splaying out slightly. See over for the same sequence viewed side-on.

2

3

whilst remaining centred, with the right shoulder moving back and round.

As the shoulders turn, an extra lever is introduced through the lifting of the arms. It's worth repeating that this is, in effect, the same swing model as in the full swing.

We like the idea of your left arm acting as a hand on a clock face. You can measure the distance of your pitches by taking your left arm back to 7 o'clock (and following through to 7), 8 (and following through to 8) or 9 or 10 o'clock. You can further add to the distances available to you, of course, by pitching with different clubs, ranging from, say, a 48-degree wedge to a 60-degree lob wedge, or by choking down on the handle. The swing mechanics, however, remain the same throughout.

On the way down, you should feel that 80 per cent of the power comes from the turning through of the torso, with 20 per cent provided by the wrists. There is a mini release. Again, feel the right hand pressing the club head down into the ball.

Your arms remain in their triangular shape until the left arm folds up (see picture 3). The wrist angles do not change.

And again, make sure you turn, both back and through! On short shots, it's so easy to get passive with the body and rely on the arms and hands. So easy – and so destructive.

1

Choking down the handle gives you an extra set of distances with each club.

Finally, turn around your spine rather than tilting your shoulders. With short clubs like wedges, you'll find yourself leaning more over the ball. From this position, it's easy to start tilting your shoulders, so that the left drops and the right rises in the backswing, and vice versa in the downswing. That's a perfect recipe for both fat and thin shots.

2

3

Turn back, rotating around the spine, while keeping the arms connected and not rolling the hands...

...and turn the core back through, again rotating around the spine. Notice the right hand has not flipped over.

WHERE 9 OUT OF 10 GOLFERS GO WRONG

What not to do: The dreaded 'scoop' – this player has kept his weight back on his right foot, tilted rather than turned, and tried to flip the ball into the air with his right hand.

What not to do: Setting up way open, with the ball off the back foot; it's a common 'method' of making the game harder than it already is.

KEEP IT SIMPLE

Bad chippers and pitchers do all sorts of things wrong. There is one common denominator, though. They all make things unnecessarily complicated.

As we've already said, they often set up way open to the ball-to-target line, with the ball wrongly positioned in the middle of the toes rather than the heels.

Often they close the club face, lead with the arms and take the club straight back, tilting their shoulders and getting very steep at the same time. That means coming back down just as steeply, inviting a fat or thin contact.

Then there are the players who favour keeping their weight on the right foot and adding a right-hand scoop in an attempt to get the ball airborne.

It's very common to see golfers failing to turn the torso at all during short shots, relying instead on their arms and hands. Their arms may travel back outside or inside the ball-to-target line but, in both cases, you can count on one thing happening – these players will roll or twist their hands to try and get the club head back on path… and then, inevitably, un-roll or un-twist them – or try to – through impact.

For such players, the sensation of trying to keep the club head outside the hands is a good one (as well as retaining the concave angle or 'cup' at the back of the left hand, as

"As with the long game, it's vital to remember one thing above all others. Hand roll is the greatest golf killer of all."

in the full swing). Try to feel that your wrists do not change position at all as the club is taken back along a straight line with the arms. As soon as the right shoulder turns back, it will bring the club inside on a mild arc. No wrist movement – none at all – is required.

As with the long game, it's vital to remember one thing above all others. Hand roll is the greatest golf killer of all.

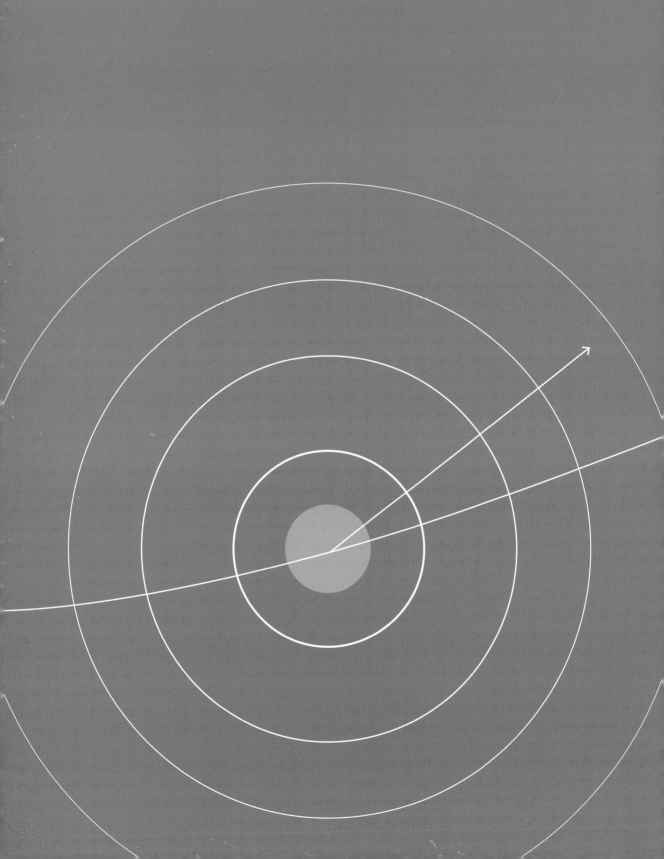

CONCLUSION

A FINAL THOUGHT

So there you have it. This is the way we see golf.

For some, it may seem an odd approach. Others may even feel that we teach the game backwards.

We prefer the term 'outwards'.

We start with the important bit – the impact zone – and work out from there.

It's what Leslie King did. It's what we do. What could be more logical than that?

Does the rest of the golf swing matter? Yes. Hugely. We'd be mad to suggest otherwise.

The transition is often highlighted as a key part of the swing, seamlessly linking the backswing and downswing. We agree. That has to be true. There are many important things that you have to do correctly to play well. If we didn't believe that, we would not bother teaching the full swing at all.

"Our method is not theoretical. It has been tried and tested over sixty years and in tens of thousands of teaching sessions."

One of the most fundamental things, though, is the impact zone.

Nothing is more important than impact. Impact is everything.

It's the only time your club touches the ball. It defines where the ball is going. You have to develop a good impact zone to play good golf. It must be an integral part of your swing.

So perhaps teaching golf 'outwards' is not so odd after all.

Think of it like this:

You are the manager of a sports team and are fortunate enough to have one of the top players in the world at your club. It doesn't take a genius to work out that this player, if they are fit, is the first name on the team sheet every week. You build the rest of the team around them.

That's how we think of the impact zone. We advise our students to get that working correctly – it is the must-have element – and then build a swing around it.

And, to continue the analogy, it's amazing how one player like, say, a Pele or a Michael Jordan starts to make the players around him perform better, too. The rest of the team feed off him. Genius rubs off.

Similarly, it's amazing how perfecting the impact zone starts to improve your backswing, downswing and throughswing. Once you know where the impact zone is, you start adjusting your route away from it and back towards it. Suddenly, your hand arc becomes smooth and regular. Suddenly, your body starts working through new positions that are consistent with the impact zone.

True, some very good golfers, against all the odds, weave a great impact zone together with a quirky backswing or downswing. Believe us, they are the exceptions. They're doing it the complicated way. Touched by genius, they are not the example for you to follow.

(Believe us too, when we say you won't ever see a good golfer with a great backswing or downswing… but a quirky impact zone!)

If your golf has not improved through the traditional method of starting at address and then methodically, sequentially working through the swing, then ask yourself why.

Could it be that you've been getting so out of position during the takeaway, backswing or downswing that you've never had a chance to learn what impact is all about?

By rebuilding your swing in this way, you will not only improve your game out of all recognition, but you will also establish a vast reservoir of knowledge to draw on in future. You will have all the checkpoints you need to get back on track on those days when things start to go wrong.

We would like to conclude by making one last thing clear. We are not exactly revolutionaries at the Knightsbridge Golf School. We've been here for a while, after all. Along with Leslie King, we don't claim to have reinvented the wheel.

What we would say is that we have developed a clearer way of observing and explaining that we pass on to our students. Our method is not theoretical. It has been tried and tested over sixty years and in tens of thousands of teaching sessions.

As we said at the start, go to any pro tournament and you will see the top players in the world starting their warm-up with mini swings. Reacquainting themselves with the be-all and end-all. The thing that makes them so good. The impact zone.

If it's good enough for them, it's certainly good enough for us – and, we'd argue, for you too.

THE FULL IMPACT ZONE

1

2

4

5

3

Let's complete this book by looking at the full impact zone, set out here in all its glory. And the impact zone is just that – glorious. It's where the real action takes place – it's where the ball gets hit. And there's nothing more glorious than a well-struck shot.

For players who fail to release, pictures 2 and 3 are key. Note how the club head is just above the hands initially, then just below them. These two frames capture the initiation of hand release, which magically increases the speed of the shaft while simultaneously allowing the club face to square up to the ball in the frames that follow (pictures 4, 5 and 6).

6

→

7

8

10

11

9

Note also how long the club face remains square, pre- and post-impact (pictures 6 through to 8). There's no dramatic closing of the face just before the strike, thus confirming that the hands are not rolling. Everything here suggests a drive straight down the fairway. There's power here too, as the final frames confirm. The accelerating club head catches up with the hands at impact, then overtakes them (pictures 8 through to 12).

Take a final look at the hands. Link their position in each picture in your mind's eye. With the arms remaining naturally extended throughout and never losing their radius, the hands are able to follow a perfect arc.

A perfect hand arc defines a perfect club head arc. And a perfect club head arc translates into a perfect result.

12

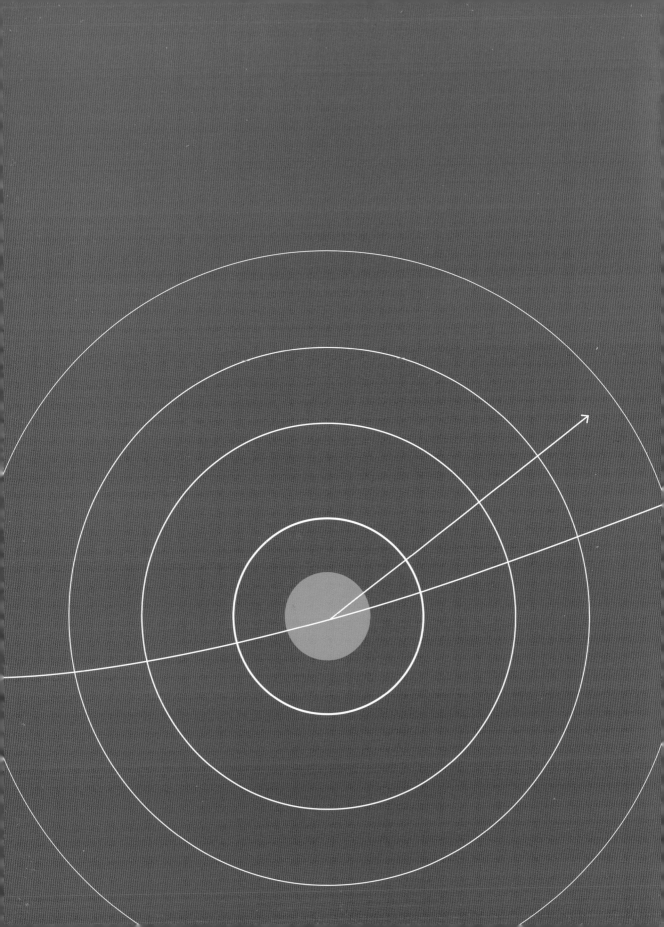

KEY PRINCIPLES

KEY PRINCIPLES

We've tried in this book to focus on what we regard as golf's major issues – complex yet crucial elements of the swing that are often overlooked, misunderstood or misinterpreted. Here, though – for the sake of completeness – are a few short observations on some of the game's basic principles which also deserve to be mentioned and reviewed.

ADDRESSING THE BALL

Line up your shots from behind the ball. Choose an intermediate target – a spot on the grass, say, just in front of the ball and on your intended line of flight. Check your grip. Walk to the side of the ball and align your club face squarely. Position your feet on a line parallel to the ball-to-target line (never position your feet before aligning the club face).

BALL POSITION

For short irons, position the ball in the centre of your stance. For long irons and fairway woods, move it a little towards your left foot. When driving – requiring an upward, sweeping blow – play the ball off the inside of the left foot.

BUNKER PLAY

Bunkers can be confusing. Golfers spend all their time perfecting impact, then, once in a bunker, they do everything they can *not to hit the ball.*

It makes sense, though. A good greenside bunker shot gets the ball into the air quickly while at the same time not going far and landing softly. You achieve this by striking the sand three or four inches behind the ball. Effectively, you are projecting a small cushion of sand out of the bunker and onto the green – with the ball perched on top.

In most respects, though, the bunker shot resembles a normal shot. Shuffle your feet down into the sand to establish a good stance, then address the ball as for a short pitch. Set up square, then flare your left foot open a little – from 12 to 11 o'clock, not 12 to 9. Don't overdo it. Place a little more weight on the left foot, as with a pitch. Flex your knees. Open the club face a little – this exposes the bounce at the bottom of your club, stopping it from cutting too deeply into the sand.

The only marked difference is ball position. Play it off your left heel. Then just swing normally, while aiming to strike the sand in the middle of your stance. The club head will cut through the sand and pick up both cushion and ball on the way through. If you play the ball too far back, you will either hit the ball first or come in too steeply, burying the club and fatting the shot.

You get the same feeling of compression in a good bunker shot as you do in your normal swing – except that the compression is against the sand, not the ball. It's still a downward strike, with your right hand pushing the club head into the sand. The downswing is a bit more forceful than normal, the body rotating a little harder to cope with the sand resistance.

There is a little wrist break, as with the pitch, but the turn creates the power. You turn through to face the target at the finish.

Poor players fixate on the ball. They can't stop themselves wanting to hit it. To avoid this, focus on the exact point where you want the club head to enter the sand. Forget the ball. It's irrelevant.

Hopefully, a lot of this sounds familiar. It's directly related to your full swing. Don't overcomplicate – this method will get you out of virtually every bunker. You don't need to stand way open, as is often taught, or swing out to in with a wide-open club face (the deepest of St Andrews' bunkers excepted).

Finally, it is important to understand that the lowest point of a swing arc comes immediately below the butt end of the club. You want this lowest point to come under the ball itself, so that the club head passes beneath the ball without hitting it.

To ensure this, press the butt slightly ahead of the ball, towards your left thigh, as you set up – just like you do while pitching. This is exactly the position you want to recreate at impact (this forward press of the hands, incidentally, will also help to open your club face a fraction). Your club head will hit the sand three or four inches behind the ball with a descending blow, and keep on descending under the ball.

> "You get the same feeling of compression in a good bunker shot as you do in your normal swing – except that the compression is against the sand, not the ball."

Poor players usually set their hands further back, with the butt positioned in the middle of the stance. Their club head enters the sand three or four inches behind the ball as well – but then starts to rise out of the sand, catching the ball thin on the way out.

GRIP

Get into your address position, set the club head on the ground, lean the shaft towards you and place your right thumb on the end of the butt. Hang your left arm down by your left side, then swing it round so that the left hand, fingers pointing downwards, meets the club palm-first.

The shaft runs diagonally across the hand, from the middle of the forefinger to the crease between the little finger and the palm. The back of the left hand faces the target. The thumb is on top of the shaft, running down the middle.

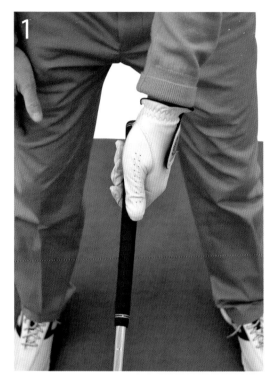

Close the fingers, then turn the hand slightly clockwise (see pictures 1 and 2), so that the left thumb stays on top of the shaft but moves just to the right of it. Looking down, you can now see two or three knuckles on the back of the left hand.

Now bring the right hand, again fingers down, onto the club, with the palm facing the target (see picture 3). The palm and the face of the club mirror each other, facing in the same direction. The right thumb wraps over the shaft, resting on its left side (see picture 4). Your right forefinger cocks up slightly and away from the other fingers to form a 'trigger'. The 'V' formed at the top of the thumb and forefinger points somewhere between your right ear and right shoulder. Looking down you can see two knuckles.

The club is held in the fingers rather than in the palms.

If a player turns his hands further clockwise, he has a 'strong' grip, further anticlockwise and it is termed a 'weak' grip.

There are various ways of bringing the hands together. In the 'Vardon' grip, used by most top players, the right little finger comes off the club and rests between the first two fingers of the left hand. Other players – for example Jack Nicklaus and Tiger Woods – used the 'interlocking' grip, intertwining the right little finger with the left forefinger. For less talented golfers,

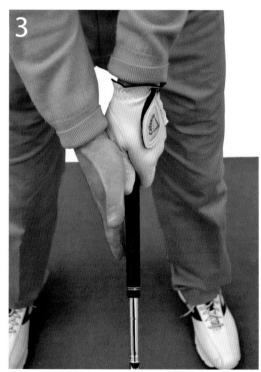

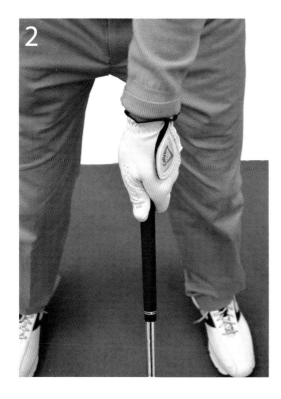

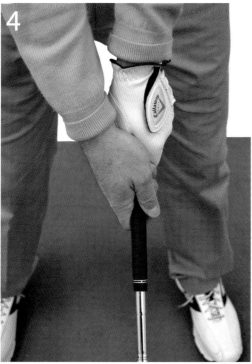

though, we feel this is a non-starter. Indeed, we call it the 'interblocking' grip, as it tends to promote a blocking action into the ball.

Then there is the 'baseball' grip, where all the fingers remain on the club. We seriously recommend you give this grip a try. In our experience, average golfers need all ten fingers on the shaft to control the club.

How hard should you grip the club? Our mentor, Leslie King, talked about 'gentle firmness'. Most students grip too hard, thus tensing their forearm muscles as well.

POSTURE
Although set-up positions vary slightly, due to players' physical characteristics and the length of the club, shoulders, hips and feet should be parallel with the ball-to-target line. The body leans forward from the hips. The back is relatively straight but not stiff. There should be no arch in the small of the back – this restricts hip and shoulder turn.

The arms hang down free of tension, about a fist's width (or slightly more for longer clubs) from the front of the thighs. The knees are slightly flexed. Your weight is evenly distributed between both legs and also across the entire sole, rather than being set in the balls of the feet or the heels. You should feel active and lively, anticipating the movement to come, like a goalkeeper preparing to face a penalty.

PUTTING

The putt is the smallest action in the game. You'll come across all sorts of styles at your club and, indeed, there are many variations among professionals too. As with the long game, though, the simplest method must, by definition, be the easiest to repeat. The most common grip is the reverse overlap, with the left forefinger draped over the fingers of the right. In putting, the club is gripped more in the palms than in the fingers. You can achieve this by holding the putter shaft more upright – do not putt using your long-game grip or by keeping your hands low. That will invite your hands to get active and the putter head to rotate too much. It has become popular to use bigger, fatter grips to help reduce hand action.

Hover the club head a fraction of an inch above the ground, ensuring the ball is struck perfectly with the sweet spot. Press the club into the ground and you will often scuff your putts or make an imperfect contact nearer the top edge of the club.

Position the ball in line with your left eye. This will mean hitting the ball on the upswing. The putting action is dominated by turning the shoulders around the spine. Use the bigger back muscles around your shoulder blades. Feel as if the right shoulder turns back to initiate the motion. Your arms and hands just hold the club in position. Tuck your elbows in against your chest to stop your arms swinging independently. Widen your stance to create stability. Keep your legs and hips solid – they do not move.

Some players try to draw the club back and through in a straight line. Theoretically, this would be ideal – if the body worked that way. We feel the club must swing on a mild arc, since your arms and shoulders rotate around the spine. This arc naturally opens the club face – just as occurs in our full swing model – although the club head remains square to your spine.

Keep the putter moving at the same tempo back and through – count 'one' during the backswing, 'two' on the way back. An overlong backswing can cause players to decelerate into impact. Some players carry out practice swings behind the ball, stopping just before contact. Don't. You're ingraining the habit of putting the brakes on.

APPENDIX

ON LEARNING GOLF – WRITER'S NOTE

This book hopefully represents Dave and Steve's teaching philosophy clearly and concisely. I was hired to help them shape their text. What I had not expected was for my own golf to improve markedly during this project.

I had some previous experience of the Knightsbridge Golf School, but spending numerous hours in Dave and Steve's company while discussing *Golf's Golden Rule* had a radical effect on my understanding of their methodology.

Not surprisingly, I felt inspired. As soon as we began work on the book I found myself spending almost as much time standing in front of a mirror – well, my French windows – as transcribing our interviews or tapping away at the laptop.

"Understand wrist hinge. Understand hand arc. Practise the positions illustrated in this book repeatedly. Practise in slow motion. Don't rush to hit balls."

I have always been fascinated with the golf swing and have always loved hitting golf balls. I had never been exposed to such knowledge or technical detail before, however. From my very first day with Dave and Steve I realised that I had never really given the moment of impact or, indeed, the impact zone, much thought. More than that, I had never properly understood how to hinge my wrists and release the club.

I had never even heard of the hand arc – despite reading umpteen instruction books over recent years. As for compression, well, that was the stuff of fairy tales. And I had never, ever, grasped the importance of my follow-through and finish.

Being with them also reminded me that hopeful ball-bashing does not equate to meaningful practice.

I was not able to spend much time playing golf while preparing this book. Nor did I receive any formal lessons at Knightsbridge. I simply whiled away many, many coffee breaks at home in front of our French windows, musing on what I was writing, swinging in ultra slow motion and working hard to ingrain the Knightsbridge basics.

My golf swing duly improved in step with the writing of the text.

We began by discussing impact and the ways the wrists work. So I worked on impact and on my wrists. We wrote about the takeaway; I practised the takeaway. We moved onto the backswing; I moved onto the backswing.

I have never been a natural. When we began, Dave politely described my swing as 'something from the 1970s'. Apparently that meant I spun my shoulders and came over the top.

I began this project as a 14-handicapper. Within four months, I had won one of three annual competitions staged at my local club, lost in the final of the second and gone down in the semi-final of the third. Along the way, I shot a 76 to defeat a 7-handicapper, while also shooting under 80 on several other occasions. By then my handicap was down to 10.9.

To finish, I would say this. Understand wrist hinge. Understand hand arc. Practise the positions illustrated in this book repeatedly. Practise in slow motion. Get a mirror (or some French windows). Don't rush to hit balls. Visit Dave and Steve. And fall in love with the disciplines of 'Golf's Golden Rule'.

Tony Lawrence

THE KNIGHTSBRIDGE GOLF SCHOOL

Should you decide to walk through the door of the Knightsbridge Golf School, you'll be following in highly accomplished footsteps.

Some of the giants of the game from all over the world have been regular visitors over the years.

Golf coaches from around the world come to 47 Lowndes Square in order to learn our systems of playing and teaching the game.

Players who have visited our school include celebrated actors and leading athletes, top businessmen and rock stars, as well as thousands of butchers, bakers and candlestick makers.

They come from all walks of life but are united in one thing – their love of this wonderful game.

We're proud to say that the vast majority of our students walk out of the school with a significantly improved game, as well as a much greater understanding of what they are trying to do when they play golf.

This fact – and the fact that our method so clearly works – gives us more joy and satisfaction than anything else.

New students often say they have never previously heard of some of the things that we teach – for example our bedrock philosophies of how to release the club correctly in the impact zone, and how to remain on the hand arc throughout the swing.

We don't know why that is. For us, these concepts are the bread and butter of golfing success.

One thing is for sure. We must be doing something right. The Knightsbridge Golf School has never relied on anything more than word of mouth to attract its clientele. Yet if there is an older, busier, more popular golf school anywhere else in the world, we have yet to hear of it. Here we are, more than half a million lessons later, about to celebrate our 60th anniversary.

At first glance, it may appear an oddity – a golf school based in some old squash courts and set right in the heart of London, with Harrods, Buckingham Palace and Big Ben as near neighbours.

Leslie King, the school's founder and one of the game's great pioneers, arrived here at the start of the 1950s.

By then, he'd spent years following golf tournaments and studying the best players of the age. With only his eyes to rely on, he scrutinised their swings, dismantled them, examined the constituent parts and then pieced them back together again until he had made sense of the game.

influence on a generation of coaches. The great American Bob Toski called him 'the godfather of the modern golf swing'. David Leadbetter also came calling.

Mr King handed the reins over to us in 1989, after we had spent many years of working as his assistants.

We've retained the foundation of what he taught and have looked to refine and develop it. We've found – and still continue to find – new ways of communicating, while supplementing our approach with state-of-the-art teaching aids, including video cameras and launch monitors.

We've taught Ryder Cup players, Walker Cup players, Solheim Cup players and Curtis Cup players, as well as amateur champions, national champions and county champions. We've coached European Tour players to victory. Like Mr King, we've also written bestselling instruction books.

Previously, the only way to learn had been through mimicry and trial by error. The swing had not yet been codified. Even the top players themselves couldn't really explain the secrets behind their success.

And, again following Mr King's example, we don't claim to have reinvented the golf swing. We just think we've made it easier and much, much quicker to learn.

Mr King, though, felt he could do just that – explain what the best golfers were doing to produce results. And, crucially, he could also tell exactly where the ball would go simply by watching someone's swing – which is why he was happy to forego an outdoor practice ground in exchange for his new subterranean home in Lowndes Square.

We hope this book will fulfil that promise and help you on the way to achieving your aims. More than that, we hope we can help you become your own coach, complete with a crystal clear understanding of what it takes to become a better player of the greatest game of all!

He led the way in establishing a comprehensive and systematic method of teaching the sport, becoming a major

Steve Gould and D.J. Wilkinson

GOLF'S GOLDEN VIDEOS

LEARN GOLF'S GOLDEN RULE
ONLINE WITH THE RENOWNED
KNIGHTSBRIDGE GOLF SCHOOL

Free video content for Golf's Golden Rule
is available online at

www.golfs-golden-rule.com

Featuring lessons from the book alongside expert
commentary from Steve Gould and D.J. Wilkinson
of the Knightsbridge Golf School, visit the website
to improve your swing even further.

The Knightsbridge Golf School can also be found
online at www.knightsbridgegolfschool.com and
you can follow the professionals on Twitter using
🐦 @KGSGolf